The Lavender Gourmet

The Lavender Gourmet

Culinary Recipes for Entertaining and Every Day

Jennifer Vasich

Foreword by Jeannie Ralston, author of The Unlikely Lavender Queen: A Memoir of Unexpected Blossoming

Moose Run
Productions

Clinton Township, Michigan

Published by...
Moose Run Productions
P.O. Box 46281 • Mount Clemens, Michigan 48046-6281
moose-run.com

© 2009 by Jennifer Vasich. All rights reserved.

Manufactured and printed in the United States of America

ISBN-13: 978-0-9766315-3-8
ISBN-10: 0-9766315-3-9

Library of Congress Control Number: 2009927990

This book is intended as a reference only. It should not be considered as personal medical advice, a medical guide, or a manual for self-treatment. All information, ingredients, and directions have been researched to ensure correctness and completeness; however, we assume no responsibility for errors, inaccuracies, or omissions.

Dedication

This book is dedicated with love to my husband, Michael, and daughter, Naomi. You are seeds of inspiration for me and bless me beyond measure!

Acknowledgments

With special thanks...

To my mother, Helen Wiley, who was a genius in the kitchen. Growing up, we never had a meal that was anything short of superb. We miss you, Mom!

To both of my older sisters, Jan and Sharon, who share Mom's talents in the kitchen, as well as her endless humor. Thank you for teaching me so much over the years and for encouraging me to complete this project.

To my mother-in-law, Mary Vasich, who is one of the most caring and giving people that I have ever met. You will always be a treasure to me.

To my editor, Nancy Feldbush, for your sharp mind and good eye. I appreciate the endless hours that you have spent to make this book a reality.

To my pastor and his wife, Pastor W.J. and Lila Davidson, for sharing your lives, for your anointed teachings, and for showing us the way to the Master. You are precious gifts from God.

To my husband Michael, who has always believed in me and fueled me to pursue my dreams—not just in business but, more important, with our family and with God.

"With God, all things ARE possible..."

The author and publisher wish to extend a hearty thank-you and say God bless you to the following people for their contributions to this cookbook.

Cover lavender field photographer: Matt Kampling

Cover photos courtesy of Heidi Bitsoli, Julie Kampling, Nancy Feldbush, Maureen Buecking & Debbie Walter

Illustrator: Debbie Walter

Copy editor: Ksenia R. Horobchenko

Proofreaders: Maribeth Criscenti, Lois Feldbush, Arlene Hicks, Julie Kampling & Marcia Swiderski

Recipe testers:
Judy Addabbo, Michelle & Richard Allen, Sharon Bacis, Kari Bacis, Heidi & Steve Bitsoli, Evelyn Bradley, Maureen Buecking, Laura Cesaro, Jessica Criscenti, Maribeth Criscenti, Diane Dueweke, Leah Dzierzawski, Bonnie Feldbush, Lois Feldbush, Nancy Feldbush, Katrina Godbout, Valerie Harms, Arlene Hicks, Julie Kampling, Tony Kampling, Sandy & Wade Leonard, Maryanne MacLeod, Mary Marlatt, Linda Mascagni, Barbara Parr, Kim Parr, Christina Schultz, Alene Soloway, David Stockton, Marcia Swiderski, Debbie Walter, Doreen Weisgerber & Jan Wiley

Contents

Delicious Lavender
by Jeannie Ralston

Soon after my husband and I started the first commercial lavender farm in Texas, I discovered something that people have known since Roman times: If there were a superlative competition among herbs, lavender easily would win the "Best All Around" title.

First, it's so beautiful to look at. Visually, rows of lavender in a field are nature's version of a pointillist work of art. Up close, every stem, every tiny bud on the pipe-cleaner-shaped flower is discernible. At middle distance, the hundreds of flowers on each plant meld into one form that suggests a pompom, and then even farther in the distance, the plants come together to create one long uninterrupted row.

Then there's that remarkable scent—sweet and hearty, potent but not overbearing. An aromatherapist I've worked with has called lavender the middle "C" of scents. Lavender, well-balanced and consistent, combines well with so many other scents—high notes like lemon and peppermint, as well as low notes such as sandalwood and jasmine. Like an effusive socialite at a party, it's a great mixer, effortlessly making friends all around.

Wonderfully for us, lavender's potency is not just experienced in our nostrils. Its powers reach far deeper, all the way down into our cerebellums. Lavender is God's gift to the anxious, the stressed, the depressed, the sleepless.

And, it turns out, to the *hungry*, as Jennifer Vasich's delightful new cookbook makes clear. The French have long appreciated lavender in cooking. Lavender is an essential part of the vaunted Herbs de Provence, along with fellow herbs basil, thyme, and fennel.

In *The Lavender Gourmet*, Jennifer showcases the versatility of lavender in contemporary cooking. Lavender adds a pleasing frisson of mystery and depth to savory dishes, such as in the recipe Lavender Chicken Florentine Stuffed Shells. It works magic with sweets too, combining deliciously with mint, citrus, cream, berries, vanilla, chocolate, and nuts (which pretty much covers the spectrum of prime dessert ingredients). My favorite dessert in Jennifer's book is the Lavender Key Lime Parfaits. I'm a sucker for Key lime pie and have been told I make a pretty good one. But, until I tried her lip-smacking recipe, I never thought about combining it with lavender—even after all my years on my lavender farm.

Jennifer's recipes are inventive and surprising that way—making you think about food combinations differently and showing even die-hard lavender lovers like me new reasons to appreciate the spectacular purple herb.

Jeannie Ralston, former owner of Hill Country Lavender in Blanco, Texas, is the author of *The Unlikely Lavender Queen: A Memoir of Unexpected Blossoming*, which recounts her journey from journalist in Manhattan to lavender farmer in rural Texas as she learns to truly "bloom where she's planted." The book was written up in *The New York Times* and recommended as a great read by *Good Morning America*. Jeannie has also been published in several magazines, including *Life*, *Time*, *National Geographic*, *Smithsonian*, *Glamour*, and *Travel & Leisure*. For more information, visit www.jeannieralston.com.

Lavender Dreams
by Jennifer Vasich

Lavender, Sweet Lavender

My love affair with lavender began a decade ago after I ordered some lavender sachets and bouquets for my natural body-care boutique in Romeo, Michigan. When the package arrived, a heavenly fragrance wafted through the air, and once the box was opened, I was transported into total lavender bliss— it was amazing. I called over everyone in the shop to experience the sweet scent that had arrived. My staff, the customers, and I truly found ourselves in a state of lavender mania. At that time, I had no idea what kind of impact lavender would have on my business and on my future, but I did know two things for sure: lavender had captivated me and I wanted to learn everything that I possibly could about the fragrant purple flower.

No other herb can compare to the allure of lavender, which has been called the "grandmother of herbs." Her leaves and blossoms beckon all who pass by, and we oblige by pinching off a sprig to enjoy her aroma. Instantly, lavender's healing oil sends us into a state of relaxation and soothes our senses. When lavender called to me, I embraced her wholeheartedly, and since then, she has comfortably settled into not only my handmade soaps and body-care products but also my gardens and culinary creations.

Over the years, as I added this culinary herb to more and more dishes, I found that everything from lemonade to roasted lamb tasted better with lavender. I never dreamed that the herb would make such a difference to the palate, but somehow, lavender's subtle sweetness takes food to a whole new dimension. This special collection of recipes, which includes old family favorites, new creations, and a wide range of culturally inspired dishes, celebrates lavender's influence on food. From my kitchen to yours, I hope you will enjoy *The Lavender Gourmet*.

Why Is Lavender So Wonderful?

Besides being a fragrant and beautiful perennial herb, lavender has another claim to fame: versatility. The word lavender is derived from the Latin "lavare," which means "to wash." Even the origin of this herb's name reveals its ability to cleanse and purify. Throughout history, people have touted lavender's benefits, including the Romans, who are recorded as being some of the first to use the herb for bathing, scenting the air, and even cooking... which is something that has only recently been discovered by those in the States.

It has also been said that certain royal dignitaries were avid lavender devotees. Folklore claims that Queen Elizabeth I expected lavender conserve at her table and that she drank lavender tea every day as a cure for her headaches. Queen Victoria, too, was noted as using lavender as a perfume, deodorant, and tonic, and Louis XIV was known for indulging in baths infused with lavender's muscle-relaxing oils. These dignitaries—and countless other people—knew what today's herbalists have confirmed: lavender's benefits are endless.

Certain constituents that are found in lavender oil have been recorded to actually calm the central nervous system, making the herb an absolute blessing to those who are affected by nervous tension. Lavender oil is also an ingredient in products that are used to help many other ailments, such as insomnia, anxiety, and muscle aches. In addition, the oil can even be rubbed on the temples and forehead to help relieve headaches. And, as Europeans have known for centuries and as those in the States are just finding out, lavender is a fantastic culinary herb!

Not only does lavender offer a delicate flavor to both sweet and savory recipes, research suggests that consuming lavender may even provide key health benefits. When someone asks for a quick, natural remedy to help soothe an upset stomach and aid digestion, mint tea is often one of the first things that comes to mind. Lavender, being a member of the mint family, delivers the same benefits. In fact, my family has found that a cup of "lavender tea"—or Soothing Lavender Tisane, which can be found on page 22—alleviates indigestion; plus, the infusion truly helps us get a restful night's sleep.

Studies show that components in the oils found in lavender may even relieve gas and bloating—a benefit that most other herbs high in volatile oils are prized for. Further research suggests that lavender is a valuable treatment for hyperactivity, insomnia, flatulence, and easing tension. One of lavender's volatile oils, linalool, has been recorded to soothe symptoms associated with asthma, cough, and respiratory problems. Linalool is also credited as an expectorant and antiseptic.

Although the benefits listed above are more predominant in the Soothing Lavender Tisane than perhaps they are in other culinary recipes, there is clearly something magnificent about using lavender in the kitchen. After trying just a few of the recipes in *The Lavender Gourmet*, one change is bound to happen in your spice rack: the containers of chives, dill, and basil will move to the side, making room for a new favorite—lavender.

Finding Organic Culinary Lavender Buds

Lavender buds are available from many sources; in fact, companies that produce bottled spices and herbs have even started offering lavender! Please see the Lavender Farm & Festival Resource Guide section, which starts on page 11, for a list of several places to purchase lavender. The Internet can also lead you to other suppliers. And, for the ultimate lavender experience, try growing your own.

Lavender in Your Backyard

Most people are surprised when I tell them lavender was the first plant that I ever gardened. I never had much success with common house plants, so I didn't believe that I could grow anything outside. My mother and grandmother were both avid gardeners, but I figured that the green thumb had somehow skipped my generation. After reading somewhere that lavender "thrived on neglect," I jokingly said to myself, "Hey! I think I could grow lavender!"

With that newfound confidence—and trusting in my husband's horticultural skills—we planted a lavender garden...not just because we wanted to but because we *needed* to. We had already hosted our second annual lavender festival at our store, and for the third year, we wanted to bring it outdoors. After all, what would an outdoor lavender festival be without lavender?

After we planted our first 100 lavender babies in the spring of 2004, we were amazed at how they flourished. We ended up with a beautiful harvest that year and learned whatever we possibly could in order to accommodate our growing Lavender Cottage Garden. I have found that lavender is quite simple to grow—as long as you follow a few basic steps. The following tips are somewhat of a beginner's guide to growing culinary lavender in your own garden. By no means is it a complete instruction manual, but it is filled with good advice that I have learned along the way. It should help you get started growing lavender successfully.

First, choose a lavender variety that is suitable for culinary recipes and one that will grow in your climate zone. It is important to remember that not all lavender varieties—there are more than 200—are suitable for cooking. Nonculinary varieties have a bitter, flowery, camphorlike taste and are not recommended for the palate. Here in Michigan, we are in zone 5, and I've had the best all-around success with the English lavenders (Lavandula angustifolia), which offer a pleasant taste to both sweet and savory dishes.

We prefer the Hidcote variety for cooking and baking because it is mild and sweet, and when used in correct amounts, it does not overpower a dish. Other English lavenders that I have liked cooking with include Jean Davis, Melissa, Munstead, and Royal Velvet. Some chefs like to use Provence (Lavandula intermedia). You may want to experiment with different varieties of lavender until you find your own personal favorite.

Next, you will want to choose a sunny area in your yard to plant your lavender—one with plenty of drainage and sandy soil. If your soil is heavy or contains clay, you can amend it by adding sand and organic compost. It is imperative that lavender plants have loose, well-drained soil. Do not mulch lavender. Mulching keeps the soil too moist around the plant, and since lavender is prone to root rot, the plants will not survive if the roots stay wet. Lavender is native to the Mediterranean...so think sandy soil and sunshine when you choose your growing location, and you should do just fine.

Lavender needs to be tended to and watered during the first year. Once the roots are established, it is very drought-tolerant and rarely needs to be watered. When it comes to fertilizer, it is best to stick with organic versions, avoiding pellet or granulated fertilizers altogether. We have had the best success fertilizing our lavender with chicken manure and organic compost. Keep in mind that lavender prefers a sweeter soil, which can be amended with lime if necessary. Organic gardening practices are important to consider, especially since the lavender will be used for culinary purposes.

When the buds are at their peak of color and a few of the florets are open along the stem, it's time to harvest. Using scissors or garden shears, cut a few stems at a time from the base of the plant. Once you have gathered enough sprigs, bind them together with a rubber band, and then hang them upside down to dry in an area that is out of direct sunlight and well ventilated. Your bundles should be dry in about two weeks. The harvested lavender buds can be used in your culinary recipes either when dry or when first harvested.

Unlike most perennials, which usually get pruned in the fall, you will want to prune your lavender in the spring just before the wood begins to turn green. This helps the plant survive even the coldest of winters. Each year, we cut the top one-third of our lavender down and round it off into a mound shape, which promotes new growth and helps the plant really flourish.

Using Organic Culinary Lavender Buds

Whether you choose to grow your own lavender or purchase organic culinary lavender buds from another source, I hope you will enjoy your culinary experience with the grandmother of herbs. When adding lavender to your own recipes, it can be ground, crushed, or left whole—it's up to you. But, remember, a little goes a long way. Always lean on the lighter side; using too much lavender in culinary recipes will overpower the other flavors. Lavender is meant to be more of a background flavor rather than one that is in the forefront.

My goal for *The Lavender Gourmet* is to introduce you to the wonderful world of culinary lavender. Although this book contains more than 140 recipes in 12 different categories, by no means would I recommend making a full-course meal with lavender in every dish. One or two recipes would be sufficient, adding that "perfect little something" to any breakfast, lunch, or dinner menu. I believe that anyone can make a gourmet meal with ease by following the recipes here, and I hope that you will enjoy them all—one at a time—for years to come.

About the Author

At one time, Jennifer Vasich thrived on living in the big city and working her way up the corporate ladder in sales and marketing. But a less metropolitan life kept beckoning, and she soon realized that she was really a country girl at heart. Always optimistic and energetic, Jennifer welcomed her new natural lifestyle with open arms and began studying massage, aromatherapy, and herbs. Along the way, she met a flowering purple herb called lavender, which altered her path once again.

After experiencing lavender's soothing qualities firsthand, Jennifer started creating and selling a line of lavender-based products in 1998. These "lavender luxuries" included handmade soaps, body-care products, teas, and culinary items. Finally, Jennifer had discovered a way to blend her passions for helping people, living a healthful life, and cooking and baking with lavender. The best part of all was that she and her husband Michael shared the same vision and passion for the lavender business.

Showering everything she touched with love and her God-given creativity, Jennifer immersed herself in lavender—which she had grown to cherish. Soon, the couple's business, Gabriel's Garden and AllThingsLavender.com, flourished. It wasn't long before Jennifer and Michael found that they had stumbled upon their true labor of love.

Never one to sit on her laurels, the ambitious yet down-to-earth "lavender lady" found a new way to share the herb's glorious characteristics. In 2002, Jennifer established the Michigan Lavender Festival. Now, every July, she and Michael host the ever-growing event, which celebrates lavender in all its splendor while showcasing the talents of Michigan-based artisans.

Jennifer's success, though, has not changed the gregarious country girl. Her faith, husband, daughter, friends, and family are still her top priorities, and she thanks God every day for the blessings in her life. This cookbook, the next step in Jennifer's efforts to reveal lavender's charms to those around her, is the best of the best of her culinary creations. She hopes it will make lavender, which calms the soul and spirit, into a favorite culinary ingredient for cooks and bakers everywhere.

Sources

Lavender: How to Grow and Use the Fragrant Herb by Ellen Spector Platt; *Lavender: Practical Inspirations for Natural Gifts, Country Crafts and Decorative Displays* by Tessa Evelegh; and *The Genus Lavandula* by Tim Upson and Susyn Andrews.

Please Note

The information presented in *The Lavender Gourmet* regarding the health benefits of lavender and other herbs is for educational purposes only. The statements contained in this book have not been evaluated by the FDA, and the information provided is not intended to diagnose, cure, or treat any disease. The results indicated may not occur in all individuals, and the benefits may vary from person to person. *The Lavender Gourmet* makes no claims or representations as to the effectiveness of lavender and other herbs in alleviating or curing any disease or condition.

Lavender Farm & Festival Resource Guide

Agri-tourism is one of the fastest growing travel trends in the United States, and lavender farms that offer tours, classes, and annual lavender festivals are certainly helping to push this movement forward.

In some regions, such as Sequim, Washington, lavender has become an important role in the sustainability of agriculture and tourism as a whole. Boasting nearly 40 farms in the Sequim-Dungeness Valley alone, the area grows more than 110,000 lavender plants each year and draws approximately 30,000 visitors for its annual lavender festival, which is held in July.

If you've never yet had the pleasure of touring a lavender field when it is in full bloom, I highly recommend that you add it to your "to do" list. Nothing can compare to the tranquility that permeates a lavender field, and the rows of streaming purple ribbons that neatly line the hills and slopes will draw you into a state of pure lavender bliss.

The following is a brief list of lavender farms and shops that offer various lavender activities and events, as well as culinary lavender.

Lavender Farms

California
The Lavender Fields
1332 Industrial Ave. • Escondido, CA 92029 • 760-839-1489
www.thelavenderfields.com

Hawaii
Ali'i Kula Lavender
1100 Waipoli Road • Kula, Maui, HI 96790 • 808-878-3004
www.aliikulalavender.com

Massachusetts
Cape Cod Lavender Farm
P.O. Box 611 • Island Pond Trail • Harwich, MA 02645 • 508-432-8397
www.capecodlavenderfarm.com

Michigan

Gabriel's Garden Lavender Boutique

111 South Main • Romeo, MI 48065 • 586-336-0418

www.allthingslavender.com

Texas

Hill Country Lavender

P.O. Box 1266 • Blanco, TX 78606 • 830-833-2294

www.hillcountrylavender.com

Lavender Farms Outside the United States

Snowshill Lavender • www.snowshill-lavender.co.uk/cm/

Lavender Festivals

Michigan

www.michlavenderfestival.com

New Mexico

www.lavenderinthevillage.com

Pennsylvania

www.palavenderfestival.com

Texas

www.blancolavenderfestival.com

Washington

www.sequimlavenderfestival.com

Lavender Lane

Basics & Beverages

Sweet Lavender

When sugar and honey are scented with the fragrance of lavender, something wonderful happens to ordinary recipes—they become tasty works of art. Just replace your granulated sugar and plain honey with these lavender-infused versions, and you'll instantly add a hint of this fabulous herb to whatever you're making. Both of these Sweet Lavender recipes are a cinch to prepare; plus, they make wonderful gifts for friends and family—just package each in a decorative glass jar, tie on ribbons and a sprig of lavender, and include a special note about these truly unique culinary treasures.

Lavender Sugar

2 cups granulated sugar
4 Tbsp Organic Culinary Lavender Buds

Photo Courtesy of Debbie Walter

Mix together the sugar and lavender buds, and place in a covered container. Store at room temperature for 1–2 weeks, shaking the container occasionally to distribute the lavender among the sugar granules. Pass the sugar through a strainer to remove the buds, and store the Lavender Sugar in an airtight container. For a more profound lavender taste, crush the lavender buds in a spice grinder or coffee grinder before mixing with the sugar, and do not remove them from the sugar.

Chef's Comments

Lavender Sugar lends a delicate floral note to recipes and makes a wonderful addition to coffee, tea, cereal, or anything that uses granulated sugar.

Lavender Honey (Infusion)

8 oz. raw light honey

4 Tbsp Organic Culinary Lavender Buds OR 8–10 sprigs of fresh lavender

Stove-Top Method

Place the honey in a small saucepan or double boiler, and cook over medium heat until the honey reaches 150°F on a candy thermometer. Do not boil; excessive heat will destroy the enzymes and other nutrients in raw honey. Remove from the heat, add the lavender buds, and stir well. Allow the flavor of the lavender buds, which will float to the top, to infuse in the honey for 6 hours or overnight. Strain out the lavender buds (to make straining easier, reheat slightly), and place the honey in a glass jar.

Sun Method

Combine the honey and lavender buds in a covered jar. Place the jar in the afternoon sun for 6 hours. Repeat for a 2nd day. If you want a more intense flavor, repeat for a 3rd day. Strain out the lavender buds (to make straining easier, reheat slightly), and place the honey in a glass jar.

Fascinating Facts

Honey is a healthful sweetener that contains vitamins, minerals, enzymes, and antioxidants. Generally, honey's taste corresponds to its color—light honey tends to have a mild taste, and dark honey, a more robust flavor. Lavender Honey tastes best when made with a light honey, such as clover, wildflower, or orange blossom.

Photo Courtesy of Debbie Walter

Recipe Tested in the Kitchen of Debbie Walter

Savory Lavender

There are hundreds of ways to create savory dishes with lavender, and one of the easiest methods is to use a spice blend containing the "grandmother of herbs." Both Lavender Lemon Pepper and Herbs de Provence are extremely versatile mixtures. They can serve as dry rubs for poultry, beef, or fish; they give marinades, soups, and stews exquisite flavor; and they season vegetables beautifully, bringing them to life.

Photo Courtesy of Nancy Feldbush

Lavender Lemon Pepper

2 Tbsp fresh-ground black pepper

2 Tbsp dried parsley

1 Tbsp Organic Culinary Lavender Buds

1 Tbsp dried minced onion

1 Tbsp lemon juice powder

1 Tbsp garlic salt

Combine all of the ingredients, and mix well. Store in an airtight container in a cool, dark location.

Chef's Comments

This seasoning blend is made with a hint of garlic, onion, and lavender—plus, it delivers a lively burst of lemon! Sprinkle it on meat or vegetables before grilling, or use it on your favorite salad. You won't believe the difference it makes.

Fascinating Facts

Herbs de Provence, also called Provençal herbs, is named for, quite literally, the region of Provence, France. Variations and recipes abound for Herbs de Provence, but to be true to its name, the fragrant blend must contain one key herb: lavender. When that lovely little flower is carefully combined with thyme, savory, rosemary, fennel seed, basil, and marjoram, the result is an aromatic mixture that infuses food with the flavor of southern France.

Herbs de Provence

1 Tbsp dried thyme

1 Tbsp dried basil

2 tsp Organic Culinary Lavender Buds

2 tsp dried rosemary

1/2 tsp fennel seed

1/2 tsp dried savory

1/2 tsp dried marjoram

Combine all of the ingredients, and mix well. Store in an airtight container in a cool, dark location.

Chef's Comments

This blend makes a wonderful gift for friends and family— simply place it in a decorative jar, and tie on some raffia. Include a recipe for using the spice mixture, and you're sure to make the recipient smile from ear to ear.

Photo Courtesy of Nancy Feldbush

Recipe Tested in the Kitchen of Nancy Feldbush

Lavender Marinades

Another way to incorporate the flavor of lavender when cooking is to use a marinade. I have a long list of fantastic lavender marinades, and I wanted to include them all—but there just wasn't room. So, with a bit of difficulty, I finally whittled my list down to these two favorites.

Lavender Lime Marinade

1/2 cup fresh-squeezed lime juice

2 Tbsp granulated sugar

2 tsp Organic Culinary Lavender Buds

1/4 tsp garlic salt

1/4 tsp fresh-ground black pepper

1 cup extra-virgin olive oil

In a small mixing bowl, combine the lime juice, sugar, lavender buds, garlic salt, and pepper. With an electric mixer, beat the mixture on low speed while slowly adding the olive oil. Store the marinade in a covered container in the refrigerator for up to 2 weeks.

Chef's Comments

This tangy marinade tastes terrific on everything from grilled meats and seafood to vegetables and salads.

For best results, marinate chicken, beef, or pork for a minimum of 2 hours (or overnight) before grilling, and baste the meat continually while cooking.

Freshly made marinades— and any portion that never came in contact with the meat—may be stored in a covered container in the refrigerator for up to 2 weeks. If the marinade has been used with a meat, please discard it.

Chef's Comments

Spice up your life with this marinade inspired by the flavors of the Caribbean. It has a little bit of heat, but it's not considered "hot."

To make an even milder marinade, decrease the amount of jalapeños—or, for some real sizzle, add more.

For best results, marinate chicken, beef, or pork for a minimum of 2 hours (or overnight) before grilling, and baste the meat continually while cooking.

Lavender Caribbean Jerk Marinade

1 cup crushed pineapple (with juice)

1/4 cup orange juice concentrate

1/4 cup fresh-squeezed lime juice

1/2 cup honey

5 jalapeño pepper slices (we use Vlasic's zesty jalapeño pepper slices)

1/4 small Vidalia onion OR other sweet onion, cut into small chunks

2 tsp Organic Culinary Lavender Buds

2 tsp ground allspice

1 tsp garlic salt

1/2 tsp cinnamon

1/2 tsp nutmeg

In a blender or food processor, combine all of the ingredients, and blend until smooth. Store the marinade in a covered container in the refrigerator for up to 2 weeks.

Recipe Tested in the Kitchen of Sharon Bacis

Soothing Lavender Tisane

It's been said that both Queen Elizabeth I and Queen Victoria treasured lavender for its many healing benefits and that Queen Elizabeth I drank an abundance of lavender tea to help relieve her migraine headaches.

Lavender tisane—or herbal infusion—is a calming, soothing beverage with a delicate floral scent and smooth flavor. Lavender has been known to help promote restful sleep; calm the central nervous system; and relieve stress, fatigue, insomnia, and congestion. It's also a good digestive aid.

Although this Soothing Lavender Tisane is delicious enough on its own, a touch of honey or fresh-squeezed lemon juice makes a wonderful addition when it is served hot.

4 Tbsp Organic Culinary Lavender Buds
2 cups cold water
1 tsp honey and/or fresh-squeezed lemon juice (optional)

Heat the water in a tea kettle. Remove the kettle from the heat once the water begins to boil. Add the lavender buds to the water, stir, and allow the herbs to steep in the kettle for 5 minutes.

Pour the lavender tisane into teacups through a strainer, and serve with 1 tsp of honey and/or fresh-squeezed lemon juice, if desired.

Chef's Comments

Lavender tisane is best when used immediately.

It can be served either hot or cold, but in order to reap all the healing benefits from the lavender, do not reheat the tisane.

Leftover tisane can be used as a facial rinse or to flavor other culinary recipes by substituting it for regular water.

Photo Courtesy of Jennifer Vasich

Recipe Tested in the Kitchen of Debbie Walter

Sparkling
Lavender Lemonade

This classic Lavender Festival favorite is now a cool, sparkling beverage! The lemon and lavender complement each other perfectly, and I've replaced the sugar with honey because of its healthful benefits and naturally sweet flavor. I hope you enjoy this delicious lemonade.

2 cups water

1 cup raw honey

2 Tbsp Organic Culinary Lavender Buds

1 cup fresh-squeezed lemon juice

2 cups sparkling water

ice cubes

lavender sprigs and lemon wedges (for garnish)

Combine the water, honey, and lavender buds in a small saucepan (it is okay if the lavender buds float on top). Over medium heat, bring the mixture to a boil. Remove from the heat as soon as the watery syrup starts to boil. Set aside, and allow the mixture to steep for 10 minutes. Strain the lavender buds from the syrup, and let it cool. Discard the lavender buds. Combine the cooled syrup and lemon juice in a pitcher. Add the sparkling water. In tall glasses, pour the Sparkling Lavender Lemonade over ice, and garnish with lavender sprigs and lemon wedges. Makes approximately 6 servings.

Chef's Comments

For best results, we recommend that you use a local raw honey, which can be found at most health food stores or gourmet food markets.

Photo Courtesy of Julie Kampling

Recipe Tested in the Kitchen of Julie Kampling

Hibiscus Lavender Lemonade

This beverage will pleasantly surprise you, and it's a perfect way to introduce culinary lavender to those who are skeptical about consuming the herb. The hibiscus flowers add a subtle sweetness to the refreshing flavor of the lavender, and both blend wonderfully with the lemonade. There is nothing like a cool glass of this lemonade on a hot summer's day, and my family has been known to enjoy it year-round!

2 cups water

2 Tbsp Organic Culinary Lavender Buds

1 Tbsp dried hibiscus flowers

1 can (6 oz. size) frozen lemonade concentrate

ice cubes

fresh lemon slices (for garnish)

In a small saucepan, boil the water, and remove from the heat. Immediately, add the lavender buds and hibiscus flowers. Stir well, and set aside, allowing the herbs to steep for 10 minutes. In a pitcher, make the lemonade according to the package's directions. After the herbs have finished steeping, strain the herbs from the water. Set aside the herbal-infused water, and discard the herbs. Add the herbal-infused water to the lemonade, and stir well. Pour over ice cubes in glasses. Garnish with fresh lemon slices, and serve. Makes approximately 2 quarts.

Photo Courtesy of Maureen Buecking

Chef's Comments

Hibiscus tea is naturally caffeine-free and loaded with vitamin C and antioxidants. It can be found at most health food stores or online at www.enjoyingtea.com.

Recipe Tested in the Kitchen of Maureen Buecking

Frozen Lavender Ginger Limeade

Ginger's pungent flavor adds a unique addition to the tart limes in this tasty drink. An amazing tonic, ginger tea has been used to help relieve cold symptoms, stomach and digestive ailments, and motion sickness. Combined with the soothing benefits of lavender, this frozen drink definitely offers more than just fabulous flavor.

2 Tbsp fresh-grated gingerroot

4 cups water

2 Tbsp Organic Culinary Lavender Buds

1 can (12 oz. size) frozen limeade concentrate (we prefer Minute Maid brand)

12–24 ice cubes

lime slices (for garnish)

Peel the ginger, and grate it with a fine-mesh grater. Heat the water to boiling, and add the gingerroot and lavender buds. Remove from the heat, and allow the ingredients to steep for 10 minutes. Strain the gingerroot and lavender buds from the water. Set aside the water, and discard the herbs.

In a 2-quart pitcher, combine the limeade and the lavender- and ginger-infused water, and stir until well blended.

Place some of the ice cubes in a blender, filling the container about halfway, then add some of the limeade mixture. The goal is to create a slush-type drink. Blend to crush the ice. Add more ice or limeade as needed until the drink is a slushy consistency. The final consistency and taste will depend on your preferences and how much ice is added.

Serve in chilled glasses with a slice of lime. Makes approximately 6–8 servings.

Photos Courtesy of Heidi Bitsoli

Recipe Tested in the Bitsoli Kitchen

Lavender Watermelon Refresher

For an exceptional beverage that is low in calories but high in taste, you can't do better than this Lavender Watermelon Refresher.

2 Tbsp Organic Culinary Lavender Buds
1 cup water
1 medium watermelon
juice from 4 limes
1 Tbsp honey
ice
lime slices or fresh mint leaves (for garnish—optional)

In a small saucepan, combine the lavender buds and water. Heat to a boil. Remove the pan from the heat as soon as the water comes to a boil. Allow the lavender buds to steep in the water for 10 minutes. Strain the lavender buds from the water. Discard the lavender buds. Place the lavender-infused water in the refrigerator to cool for at least 1 hour.

In the meantime, remove the seeds and pulp from the watermelon. Discard the seeds and rind. Place the watermelon pulp, lime juice, cooled lavender-infused water, and honey into a food processor or blender. Pulse until the watermelon is smooth. Pour the juice into glasses filled with ice, and garnish with lime slices or fresh mint leaves, if desired. Makes approximately 8–10 servings.

Photo Courtesy of Nancy Feldbush

Recipe Tested in the Kitchen of Nancy Feldbush

Minty Lavender Tea Punch

*This herbaceous punch offers a cool respite on a summertime afternoon.
The lemon and orange flavors enhance the herbs, making a thirst-quenching
beverage that you and your guests are sure to enjoy.*

2 Tbsp fresh mint leaves OR 2 tsp dried mint leaves

2 Tbsp Organic Culinary Lavender Buds

3 cups cold water, plus 5 cups, separated

1 cup granulated sugar

1 1/4 cups orange juice

1/3 cup fresh-squeezed lemon juice

fresh lemon or orange slices (for garnish—optional)

fresh mint or lavender sprigs (for garnish—optional)

wire-mesh tea ball OR muslin tea bag

Place the mint and lavender buds into a wire-mesh tea ball or muslin tea bag,
and set aside. Boil 3 cups of the water, and then place the wire-mesh tea ball
or muslin tea bag into the boiling water. Remove the water from the heat, and
allow the herbs to steep for about 8 minutes.

Remove the tea ball or tea bag, and discard the herbs. Add the sugar to the tea,
and stir until dissolved. Stir in the orange juice, lemon juice, and remaining
5 cups of cold water. Mix well. Serve over ice, and garnish with fresh
lemon or orange slices and fresh mint or lavender sprigs, if desired. Makes
approximately 8–12 servings.

Photo Courtesy of Heidi Bitsoli

Recipe Tested in the Bitsoli Kitchen

Lavender Blackberry Punch

This sparkling beverage has a distinctive berry flavor with a hint of lavender and spice. My family and I enjoy it with brunch, but it also makes an impeccable punch to serve alongside a holiday buffet.

4 cups blackberries, fresh OR frozen

1 1/2 cups water

1 cup granulated sugar

1 tsp whole cloves

1 tsp whole allspice

1 cinnamon stick (3 inch size), broken in half

2 tsp Organic Culinary Lavender Buds

1 bottle (2 liter size) Vernor's brand ginger ale soda (if you prefer, a lemon-lime soda can be used instead of the ginger ale)

fresh OR frozen blackberries (for garnish—optional)

wire-mesh tea ball OR muslin tea bag

Place the blackberries into a large pot, and crush them. Add the water to the crushed blackberries. Bring the mixture to a boil, reduce the heat to medium-low, and simmer for 10 minutes. Strain the blackberries through a wire-mesh strainer, keeping the juice and discarding the pulp. Pour the juice back into the pot, add the sugar, and stir.

Place the 4 spices—cloves, allspice, cinnamon, and lavender buds—into a wire-mesh tea ball or muslin tea bag, and then add it to the blackberry juice. Heat the juice and the spices to a simmer, and cook, uncovered, for 25 minutes. Remove the ball or bag, and discard the spices. Cool the juice completely. What you now have is a blackberry concentrate.

When serving the Lavender Blackberry Punch, fill a glass with ice, and mix one part of the blackberry concentrate with two parts of the soda. Garnish with fresh or frozen blackberries, if desired. Any unused concentrate may be refrigerated for up to 1 week. Makes approximately 10–12 servings.

Photo Courtesy of Nancy Feldbush

Recipe Tested in the Kitchen of Arlene Hicks

Peach Nectar & Lavender Ice Tea

The combination of peach nectar and lavender tea creates a lovely cold beverage. This ice tea makes a distinguished addition to special occasions and tastes dreamy on a hot day.

3 cups cold water, plus 3 cups, separated

2 Tbsp Organic Culinary Lavender Buds

2 Earl Grey tea bags

1/2 cup granulated sugar

2 containers (11–11.5 oz. size) peach nectar

1/4 cup fresh-squeezed lemon juice

a fresh sprig of lavender (for garnish—optional)

In a small saucepan, combine 3 cups of the cold water along with the lavender buds and tea bags. Bring the water to a boil. Once it begins to boil, reduce the heat to low, and simmer the lavender buds and tea for 10 minutes.

Remove the pan from the heat. Take out the tea bags, and strain the lavender buds from the water. Discard the lavender buds and tea bags. Return the herbal-infused water to the pan, and add the sugar, stirring until the sugar is completely dissolved.

In a large pitcher, combine together the peach nectar, remaining 3 cups of cold water, lavender and tea infusion, and lemon juice. Stir well. Serve over ice, and garnish with a fresh sprig of lavender, if desired. Makes approximately 6–8 servings.

Photo Courtesy of Marcia Swiderski

Recipe Tested in the Kitchen of Marcia Swiderski

Lavender Mocha Latte

The rich, dark chocolate espresso in this latte is exquisitely balanced by the slightly sweet taste of the lavender-infused milk. And, when topped with fresh whipped cream and a dash of cocoa powder, nothing compares to it.

3 1/4 cups low-fat milk

1 Tbsp Organic Culinary Lavender Buds

2/3 cup bittersweet chocolate chips (we prefer Ghirardelli chips)

2 Tbsp instant espresso (instant coffee may be used instead)

1 tsp vanilla extract

sweetener (to taste)

fresh whipped cream and cocoa powder (for garnish—optional)

In a medium-size saucepan, stir together the milk and lavender buds. Cook over medium heat just until the milk begins to bubble. Remove the pan from the heat, stir, and allow the lavender buds to steep in the milk for 10 minutes. Strain the lavender buds from the milk. Discard the lavender buds. Return the lavender-infused milk to the saucepan.

Add the chocolate chips, espresso, and vanilla extract to the lavender-infused milk, and stir. Cook the mixture over low heat until the chocolate is completely melted. Sweeten to taste, and pour evenly into 4 mugs. Top with fresh whipped cream and lightly dust with cocoa powder, if desired. Serve immediately. Makes approximately 4 servings.

Variation

Add 1 tsp cherry extract instead of the vanilla extract, and top with whipped cream, shaved chocolate, and a cherry for a Lavender Black Forest Latte.

Photo Courtesy of Marcia Swiderski

Recipe Tested in the Kitchen of Diane Dueweke

Lavender Lane

Breakfast & Brunch

Lavender Apple Raisin Dumplings

These appetizing apple dumplings are surprisingly simple to make and taste wonderful served with fresh whipped cream or vanilla yogurt. Any variety of apples may be used, but a firm baking apple is recommended.

2 apples, peeled and cored

1 pkg (8 oz. size) refrigerated crescent rolls

4 Tbsp butter

1/4 cup granulated sugar

2 Tbsp packed brown sugar

2 tsp Organic Culinary Lavender Buds

1/2 tsp cinnamon

1/4 cup raisins

1/4 cup pecans, finely chopped

Preheat the oven to 350°F. Generously spray a 9-inch round or square baking dish with nonstick cooking spray.

Cut the apples in quarters. Wrap each apple quarter with a section of the crescent roll dough. Place the dumplings into the prepared baking dish.

In a small saucepan, melt the butter, and add both sugars, along with the lavender buds and cinnamon. Stir until blended. Pour the sugar mixture over the dumplings, and sprinkle with the raisins and chopped pecans.

Bake at 350° for 30 minutes. Let the dumplings cool for 10 minutes before serving. Serve with fresh whipped cream or vanilla yogurt, and top with any sauce, raisins, or pecans that remain in the baking dish. Makes 8 servings.

Photo Courtesy of Debbie Walter

Recipe Tested in the Kitchen of Debbie Walter

Apple Cinnamon Rolls with Lavender Vanilla Icing

There's nothing quite like waking up to the scent of cinnamon rolls baking in the oven, and with this simple recipe, you can have that wonderful experience anytime! These delicious rolls are a cinch to prepare, and they taste absolutely marvelous with my Lavender Vanilla Icing.

1 loaf (1 pound size) frozen bread dough

1/2 cup butter, softened

1 1/2 cups apples, peeled, cored, and chopped (Gala, Golden Delicious, or Jonathan apples work the best)

1/3 cup pecans, finely chopped (optional)

Cinnamon and Sugar Blend

1/4 cup granulated sugar

1/2 cup packed brown sugar

1 Tbsp cinnamon

1/2 Tbsp nutmeg

Topping

Lavender Vanilla Icing (see the recipe on the next page)

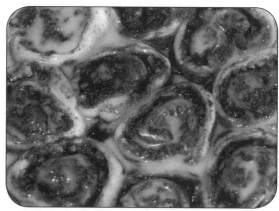

Photo Courtesy of Julie Kampling

Thaw the bread dough according to the package's directions. The dough does not need to rise at this point; it just needs to be thawed. Preheat the oven to 350°F. Gently shape the dough into a 9-inch x 12-inch rectangle. Spread the butter over the dough, and evenly distribute the apples and pecans, if desired, over the buttered dough. Sprinkle the Cinnamon and Sugar Blend on the top.

Starting at the 9-inch side, roll up the rectangle of dough from end to end. Using a sharp knife, slice the roll into 12 pinwheel-looking pieces. Place the rolls, evenly spaced, in a well-greased or nonstick 9-inch x 13-inch baking dish or pan. The rolls should be placed so the pinwheel is facing up.

Cover the pan of rolls with a clean, slightly dampened dish towel, and let the dough rise for about 30 minutes. Remove the towel just before baking. Bake at 350° for about 15–20 minutes or until the rolls are a light brown. Allow the rolls to cool slightly, and drizzle with Lavender Vanilla Icing. Serve warm. Makes approximately 10–12 rolls.

Lavender Vanilla Icing

6 Tbsp milk

3 tsp lavender buds

2 Tbsp butter, softened

1/8 tsp salt

1/4 tsp vanilla extract

2 cups powdered (confectioners') sugar

In a microwave-safe bowl, add the milk and lavender buds, and heat in the microwave for 20 seconds on high power. Allow the lavender buds to steep in the milk for 15 minutes. Strain the lavender buds from the milk, and discard the lavender buds. Return the lavender-infused milk to the bowl. Add the remaining ingredients to the milk, and beat with an electric mixer until smooth. If necessary, add a touch more of either milk or powdered sugar until the icing is the consistency that you prefer.

Recipe Tested in the Kitchen of Julie Kampling

Lavender Black Raspberry Danish

Mascarpone cheese (pronounced mas-car-POH-neh) is a soft, buttery Italian cream cheese that tastes much like Devonshire cream. And, when added to the sweet tartness of black raspberry preserves and the gentle aroma of lavender, it creates a delicious pastry that tempts the senses.

1 pkg (2 sheet size) frozen puff pastry (we prefer Pepperidge Farm brand)

1 large egg yolk

3/4 cup mascarpone cheese

1/4 cup granulated sugar, plus 2 tsp

1/2 tsp vanilla extract

2 Tbsp all-purpose flour

1 tsp sea salt

1/3 cup black raspberry preserves

2 tsp Organic Culinary Lavender Buds

Egg Wash

1 egg

2 Tbsp water

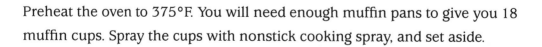

Preheat the oven to 375°F. You will need enough muffin pans to give you 18 muffin cups. Spray the cups with nonstick cooking spray, and set aside.

Thaw the puff pastry according to the package's directions. Cut each sheet into 9 squares. Place the puff pastry squares on a counter or cutting board lined with parchment paper. Firmly flatten each square with a pastry roller or your hand until the pastry resembles a very thin pancake. Gently place each puff pastry square into the prepared muffin cups.

In a medium-size mixing bowl, beat together the egg yolk, mascarpone cheese, sugar, and vanilla extract. Add the flour and salt; blend until smooth. Set aside. In a separate bowl, mix the black raspberry preserves with the lavender buds.

Spoon about 3/4 Tbsp of the cheese filling into the center of each pastry square. Next, place about 1 tsp of the fruit preserves mixture on top of the cheese mixture. Gently lift up the four corners of each pastry square, and press them together to seal.

To make the egg wash, place the egg in a small bowl, and beat lightly with a fork. Add the 2 Tbsp of water and beat until well mixed. Using a pastry brush, wipe the egg wash on each pastry.

Bake at 375° for 15–20 minutes or until the tops are a nice golden brown. Allow to cool completely before serving. Makes 18 Danish pastries.

Recipe Tested in the Kitchen of Marcia Swiderski

Almond Coffee Cake with Lavender Almond Glaze

This impressive coffee cake really steals the show at brunch. The almond filling tastes exceptional when paired with the lavender glaze. After one bite, you'll know the extra work involved in preparing the dough the day before was well worth the effort.

Coffee Cake
1/2 cup sour cream
1/4 cup butter
1/2 tsp salt
1 pkg (1/4 oz. size) active dry yeast
1/4 cup granulated sugar
1/4 cup very warm water
1 egg, well-beaten
2 cups all-purpose flour

Filling
1 can (8 oz. size) almond paste
1/4 cup blanched almonds, ground
4 Tbsp unsalted butter, softened
1 Tbsp granulated sugar
1 egg

Glaze
Lavender Almond Glaze (see the
    recipe on the next page)
toasted almond slices (for garnish)

In a saucepan, combine together the sour cream, butter, and salt. Cook over medium-low heat, stirring constantly, for about 5 minutes. Remove from the heat, and cool to room temperature. In a mixing bowl, dissolve the yeast and sugar in the warm water. Allow the yeast to bubble for at least 5 minutes. Add the sour cream mixture and egg, mixing well. Gradually stir in the flour until the ingredients are well blended—the dough will be very soft. Cover, and refrigerate overnight.

The next day, combine together all of the ingredients for the filling in a medium-size mixing bowl, and beat with an electric mixer until smooth, about 4–5 minutes. Set aside. On a lightly floured surface, knead the chilled dough, folding over 6–7 times. Divide the dough in half, and roll each half into an 8-inch x 12-inch rectangle. Spread half of the filling over each rectangle, keeping it about 1 inch away from all the edges. Roll the dough up in a jelly roll fashion, starting from the long side. Pinch together the dough at the seams and at the ends to seal.

Place both dough rolls, seam sides down, on a well-greased baking sheet. Cut about 5 crosswise slits, each about 2 inches long, in the top of each coffee cake. Cover, and let the dough rolls rise in a warm spot for about 1 hour or until they double in size. Preheat the oven to 375°F. Bake the coffee cakes at 375° for 20–25 minutes or until the tops are golden brown. Cool on a wire rack, and top with the Lavender Almond Glaze. Sprinkle with toasted almond slices. Makes 2 loaves, yielding approximately 10–12 servings total.

Lavender Almond Glaze

5 Tbsp milk
3 tsp lavender buds
2 Tbsp butter, softened
1/8 tsp salt

1/4 tsp almond extract
2 cups powdered (confectioners') sugar

Photo Courtesy of Debbie Walter

In a microwave-safe bowl, add the milk and lavender buds, and heat in the microwave for 20 seconds on high power. Allow the lavender buds to steep in the milk for 15 minutes. Strain the lavender buds from the milk, and discard the lavender buds. Return the lavender-infused milk to the bowl. Add the remaining ingredients to the milk, and beat with an electric mixer until smooth. If necessary, add a touch more of either milk or powdered sugar until the glaze is the consistency that you prefer.

Recipe Tested in the Kitchen of Debbie Walter

Nutty Pancakes with Lavender Maple Caramel Sauce

From the wholesome crunch of pecans and almonds to the sweet Lavender Maple Caramel Sauce, these pancakes are real crowd-pleasers. They are also delicious served with fresh strawberries and cream, but my family is partial to the buttery flavor of the sauce.

1 cup buttermilk (regular milk may be used instead)

1 large egg

1 cup "JIFFY" all-purpose baking mix

2 Tbsp quick-cooking oats

1/4 cup whole wheat flour

2 Tbsp wheat bran

1/4 cup pecans, finely chopped

1/4 cup almonds, slivered

butter (for frying)

Lavender Maple Caramel Sauce (see the recipe on the next page)

Pour the buttermilk into a bowl, and then whisk in the egg. Gradually add the baking mix, oats, wheat flour, and wheat bran. Mix until well blended. Fold in the pecans and almonds. To bake the pancakes, spoon small amounts of the mixture onto a hot-buttered griddle. Turn the pancakes when the baking side has browned, and then brown the other side. Serve with Lavender Maple Caramel Sauce. Makes approximately 7–8 pancakes (4 inch size).

Lavender Maple Caramel Sauce

1 cup 100% pure maple syrup

2 Tbsp granulated sugar

2 Tbsp butter

1/2 cup light cream

3 Tbsp Organic Culinary Lavender Buds

In a medium-size saucepan, stir together all of the ingredients, and cook over medium-high heat until the mixture comes to a boil. Reduce the heat to low, and cook for 5 minutes, stirring often. Remove from the heat, and cool slightly. Strain the lavender buds from the sauce, and discard the lavender buds. Serve the warm sauce over our Nutty Pancakes or your favorite pancakes or waffles.

Cover, and refrigerate any unused portion of the sauce for up to 1 week. Reheat and mix well before using.

Chef's Comments

Lavender Maple Caramel Sauce is also excellent when served over ice cream!

Photo Courtesy of Debbie Walter

Recipe Tested in the Kitchen of Debbie Walter

Sweet Crepes with Lavender Berry Compote

Crepes, a part of traditional French cuisine, are very thin pancakes made with a few simple ingredients. The crepes in this recipe are filled with a crème filling and topped with a scrumptiously sweet berry compote. These Sweet Crepes with Lavender Berry Compote are impeccable when served as a light breakfast or even as a dessert.

Crème Filling

1 container (8 oz. size) mascarpone cheese OR cream cheese
2 Tbsp milk
1/2 tsp vanilla extract
2 cups powdered (confectioners') sugar

To make the crème filling, in a medium-size mixing bowl, beat together the cheese, milk, and vanilla extract with an electric mixer on medium speed until light and fluffy. Reduce the mixer's speed to low, and slowly add the powdered sugar. Continue mixing until well incorporated. Increase the speed to medium, and beat until smooth. Refrigerate until ready to use.

Crepes

1 cup all-purpose flour
2 Tbsp granulated sugar
2 eggs
1 1/4 cups low-fat milk
1 Tbsp melted butter, plus 2 Tbsp for frying
1/2 tsp vanilla extract

To make the crepes, sift the flour into a bowl, and add the sugar. Make a well in the middle of the dry ingredients, and add the eggs, milk, and butter. With an electric mixer, blend well until the batter is the consistency of a light cream. Add the vanilla extract, and mix until well blended. Place the batter in the refrigerator for about 1 hour.

Over medium heat, add a small nub of butter to a crepe pan or a small nonstick frying pan. When the butter bubbles around the edges, pour in enough of the crepe batter to lightly cover the bottom of the pan. Swirl the pan around to spread out the batter. (If you added too much batter, pour the excess back into the bowl immediately.)

Cook the batter until the edges of the crepe become slightly browned and the top is dry. Gently flip the crepe over to brown the other side. Treat the first crepe as a test, since the first crepe rarely turns out properly! Continue until all the batter is used. Place the crepes on a plate, and cover with a clean kitchen towel to keep them warm.

Lavender Berry Compote

1/2 cup fresh-squeezed orange juice
1 Tbsp Organic Culinary Lavender Buds
1/4 cup water
2 tsp sugar
4 cups frozen mixed berries, thawed
pinch of salt

To make the berry compote, in a medium-size saucepan, combine the orange juice, lavender buds, water, and sugar over medium heat. Bring to a boil, stirring to dissolve the sugar. Cook for 2 minutes. Reduce the heat to low, and add the berries and salt. Continue to cook over low heat for 3–5 minutes, stirring and breaking up the berries. Remove from the heat, and cover to keep warm.

Filling the Crepes

Take a heaping spoonful of the crème filling, and spread it in the middle of each crepe. Fold the crepes in thirds, and place on individual plates. Two or three crepes per person is usually best. Placing all of the crepes on a large serving platter also makes a nice presentation. Spoon 1–2 Tbsp of the berry compote over each crepe. Serve immediately. Makes approximately 8 servings.

Chef's Comments

For a reduced-fat version, replace the crème filling with low-fat cottage cheese.

Recipe Tested in the Kitchen of Arlene Hicks

Savory Crepes with Lavender, Mushrooms & Bacon

Paris is a mecca for "creperies," or crepe stands, and everyone seems to have a favorite. My siblings and I grew up on crepes, and our mother's best-loved recipe was one for "crepes suzette," which was baked in the oven and contained a filling made of cottage cheese, sugar, and cinnamon. Although there are hundreds of variations for crepes, this savory recipe is sure to have you dreaming in French. Bon appétit!

Crepes
1 cup all-purpose flour
2 Tbsp granulated sugar
2 eggs
1 1/4 cups low-fat milk
1 Tbsp melted butter, plus 2 Tbsp for
    frying
1/2 tsp vanilla extract

To make the crepes, sift the flour into a bowl, and add the sugar. Make a well in the middle of the dry ingredients, and add the eggs, milk, and butter. With an electric mixer, blend well until the batter is the consistency of a light cream. Add the vanilla extract, and mix until well blended. Place the batter in the refrigerator for about 1 hour.

Over medium heat, add a small nub of butter to a crepe pan or a small nonstick frying pan. When the butter bubbles around the edges, pour in enough of the crepe batter to lightly cover the bottom of the pan. Swirl the pan around to spread out the batter. (If you added too much batter, pour the excess back into the bowl immediately.)

Cook the batter until the edges of the crepe become slightly browned and the top is dry. Gently flip the crepe over to brown the other side. Treat the first crepe as a test, since the first crepe rarely turns out properly! Continue until all the batter is used. Place the crepes on a plate, and cover with a clean kitchen towel to keep them warm.

Mushroom and Bacon Filling

5 strips bacon

1 Tbsp unsalted butter, plus 2 Tbsp, separated

1 pkg (8 oz. size) sliced mushrooms

2 Tbsp all-purpose flour

2 cups low-fat milk

3 Tbsp fresh-grated Parmesan cheese

1/3 cup sour cream

2 Tbsp green onion, chopped

1 Tbsp fresh parsley, chopped

1 tsp Organic Culinary Lavender Buds

a pinch of fresh-ground black pepper

additional fresh-grated Parmesan cheese and a sprig of parsley (for garnish—optional)

To make the filling, in a large skillet, cook the bacon until crisp. Place the cooked bacon on a cookie sheet lined with paper towels to absorb any fat. Allow the bacon to cool, crumble, and set aside. Discard the fat from the skillet. Add 1 Tbsp of butter to the skillet, and sauté the mushrooms over medium-high heat until they are a light golden brown. Remove the skillet from the heat.

To make a "roux" for the filling, melt the remaining 2 Tbsp of butter in a small saucepan over medium-high heat, and add the flour. While stirring constantly with a wire whisk, continue to cook over medium heat for 3 minutes. Gradually add the milk, whisking constantly, and cook for 4–7 minutes until smooth. Reduce the heat to low, add the Parmesan cheese and sour cream to the roux, and stir until the ingredients are well incorporated. Continue to simmer over low heat, stirring occasionally, until the sauce thickens.

Spoon 1/3 of the sauce into a small bowl, cover, and set aside. Add the bacon, mushrooms, green onion, parsley, lavender buds, and pepper to the remaining 2/3 of the sauce, and stir until well blended.

Filling the Crepes

Preheat the oven to 250°F. To fill a crepe, take 1/4 cup of the bacon and mushroom filling, and spread it in the middle of the crepe. Fold the crepe in thirds, and place it in an ovenproof baking dish. Repeat until all of the crepes are stuffed. Pour the reserved sauce over the crepes, cover, and bake at 250° for 15 minutes or until heated through. Garnish with additional fresh-grated Parmesan cheese and a sprig of parsley, if desired, and serve. Makes approximately 8 servings.

Recipe Tested in the Bitsoli Kitchen

Banana Nut French Toast with Lavender Honey Butter

Several years ago, my sister Sharon treated me to a "girls' weekend getaway" in Manistee, Michigan, at a quaint little bed-and-breakfast near Lake Michigan. We thoroughly enjoyed our relaxing weekend, and while there, the innkeepers made an incredible breakfast that included French toast with a sumptuous banana-nut filling. The recipe here is my own version of that decadent breakfast, and it tastes absolutely amazing when served with homemade Lavender Honey Butter.

3 ripe bananas, peeled and mashed

3 eggs, slightly beaten

3/4 cup milk

1 tsp vanilla extract

1/4 cup packed brown sugar

1/4 tsp cinnamon

1/4 tsp ground nutmeg

butter (for frying)

10–12 slices French bread (preferably day-old slices 1/2-inch-thick)

Lavender Honey Butter (see the recipe on the next page)

1 cup walnuts, finely chopped

powdered (confectioners') sugar (for dusting—optional)

Beat together the banana, eggs, milk, vanilla extract, brown sugar, cinnamon, and nutmeg with an electric mixer until well blended.

Melt a nub of butter in large skillet over medium-high heat. Dip each piece of bread into the batter, and coat both sides evenly. Place the bread in the skillet, turning once, until brown on both sides.

Serve with Lavender Honey Butter, and sprinkle with chopped walnuts. The slices can also be dusted with powdered sugar, if desired. Makes approximately 6–8 servings.

Lavender Honey Butter

2 sticks butter, softened
1/4 cup honey
1 tsp Organic Culinary Lavender Buds

In a medium-size mixing bowl, whip together the ingredients until light and fluffy. Remove the butter from the bowl, and spoon onto parchment paper or plastic wrap. Form into a log, and refrigerate for 2 hours before using. Store the Lavender Honey Butter in an airtight container, and refrigerate for up to 2 weeks. Makes approximately 1 cup.

Chef's Comments

To make the Lavender Honey Butter without the lavender buds in the finished product, simply substitute 1/4 cup of prepared Lavender Honey (see the recipe on page 17) for the plain honey and lavender buds.

Recipe Tested in the Kitchen of Michelle & Richard Allen

Egg Omelet with Herbs & Goat Cheese

Besides being light and flavorful, this simple omelet contains naturally good ingredients. It's a no-fuss recipe that I like to make in the summer when fresh herbs and garden vegetables are plentiful.

4 eggs

salt (to taste)

fresh-ground black pepper (to taste)

1 tsp grapeseed oil

2 shiitake mushrooms, sliced and broiled to soften

1 small tomato, seeded and diced

1/8 tsp Organic Culinary Lavender Buds

1/4 tsp fresh rosemary, chopped

1/4 tsp fresh basil, chopped

3 Tbsp crumbled goat cheese OR feta cheese

fresh herbs (for garnish)

Place the eggs in a large mixing bowl, and whisk vigorously until well blended and frothy. Season with salt and pepper, to taste.

Heat a large omelet pan over medium-high heat. Once the pan is hot, add the grapeseed oil, eggs, mushrooms, and tomato. Stir the eggs, and concentrate on moving them from the outside of the pan to the center. Sprinkle the herbs on the eggs, and continue to cook until the eggs are set.

Once the omelet is cooked, remove the pan from the heat, and sprinkle the cheese on top. Place the omelet under a broiler for about 1 minute, watching carefully to prevent burning, until the cheese melts. Roll the omelet in half, and serve immediately. Garnish with fresh herbs, and serve with breakfast potatoes, if desired. Makes approximately 2–4 servings.

Photo Courtesy of Tony Kampling

Recipe Tested in the Kitchen of Tony Kampling

Basil & Lavender Breakfast Strata

My easy Basil & Lavender Breakfast Strata has been a family favorite for many years. The basil and lavender add a grand flavor to this "oven omelet," which is filling enough to serve by itself. To save on time, this dish can be easily prepared the night before. To finish it, simply remove from the refrigerator, and bake!

1 pkg (8 oz. size) ground-turkey sausage

6 eggs

7 slices day-old bread, cut into cubes

2 cups low-fat milk

1/2 cup (4 oz.) low-fat cream cheese, melted

1 cup cheddar cheese, shredded

1 pkg (8 oz. size) sliced mushrooms

1 pkg (10 oz. size) frozen asparagus, thawed and drained

1/2 cup Vidalia onion OR other sweet onion, minced

1 Tbsp butter, melted

1 Tbsp fresh basil, chopped OR 2 tsp dried basil

1/2 tsp Organic Culinary Lavender Buds

1/4 tsp fresh-ground black pepper

1/2 tsp salt

In a large skillet, brown the sausage, drain, and set aside. In a large mixing bowl, beat together the eggs. Add the remaining ingredients, along with the sausage, and mix well.

Spoon the mixture into a well-buttered 9-inch x 13-inch baking dish. Cover, and refrigerate for 8 hours or overnight.

Preheat the oven to 350°F. Bake the strata, uncovered, at 350° for 60–70 minutes or until a knife inserted near the center comes out clean. Refrigerate any leftovers. Makes approximately 6–8 servings.

Chef's Comments

If you happen to be using a glass baking dish for the strata, allow the dish to warm up to room temperature before placing it in the preheated oven. The extreme temperature change can cause a glass dish to break.

Photo Courtesy of Richard Allen

Recipe Tested in the Kitchen of Michelle & Richard Allen

Lavender, Wild Mushroom & Swiss Quiche

For a perfect Sunday brunch, try serving my Lavender, Wild Mushroom & Swiss Quiche with hot tea and a side of fresh fruit. Using ready-made piecrusts makes this dish a cinch to prepare, but if you'd prefer to make your own crust, try the recipe for the tart pastry that is used in my Luscious Strawberry & Lavender Cream Tart, which can be found on page 244.

2 unbaked piecrusts (9 inch size)

2 Tbsp butter

1 cup yellow onion, finely minced

1 garlic clove, finely minced

1 pkg (8 oz. size) sliced mushrooms

1/2 tsp salt

1/8 tsp fresh-ground black pepper

1/4 tsp Organic Culinary Lavender Buds

1/4 tsp dried rosemary

4 large eggs

1 1/2 cups light cream

2 Tbsp all-purpose flour

2 cups Swiss cheese, shredded

Remove the piecrusts from any packaging, and set aside.

In a medium-size pan, heat the butter over medium-low heat, and sauté the onion and garlic for 4 minutes. Add the mushrooms, salt, pepper, lavender buds, and rosemary. Continue sautéing for another 5–7 minutes. Remove the pan from the heat, and set aside.

In a medium-size mixing bowl, combine together the eggs, cream, and flour. With an electric mixer set at medium-high speed, mix until the eggs become frothy.

Preheat the oven to 375°F.

Sprinkle half of the Swiss cheese over the bottom of the piecrusts, and then spread the mushroom mixture over the cheese, dividing it evenly between the two crusts. Sprinkle the other half of the cheese over the top of the mushrooms, and pour the egg mixture on top of it all, again dividing everything evenly between the two crusts.

Bake at 375° for 35–45 minutes or until the center is firm. Cool for 15 minutes before serving. This quiche is best served warm or at room temperature. Makes 2 quiche (9 inch size), yielding approximately 10–14 servings total.

Recipe Tested in the Kitchen of Diane Dueweke

Cheesy Herb Potato Bake

This potato casserole makes a remarkable companion for your favorite omelet or a great side dish at dinnertime. And, to transform it into a main course, top with any variety of fresh vegetables just before serving— mushrooms, red and green peppers, diced tomatoes, and jalapeños are all scrumptious.

1 Tbsp butter

1/2 cup onion, minced

1/2 cup milk

1/2 cup (4 oz.) cream cheese

1/4 cup beef stock or other broth

1/4 tsp garlic powder

1/2 tsp sea salt

1/4 tsp fresh-ground black pepper

1 tsp Herbs de Provence (with lavender)

4 cups frozen Ore-Ida southern style hash browns

1 cup Colby cheese, shredded

Preheat the oven to 425°F.

In a medium-size soup pot, heat the butter over medium heat, and sauté the onion for about 4–6 minutes. Add the milk, cream cheese, beef stock, garlic powder, salt, pepper, and Herbs de Provence, and mix well. Continue to heat, stirring frequently, just until the cream cheese melts.

Remove from the heat, and add the remaining 2 ingredients. Mix well again.

Transfer the potato mixture to a well-greased, ovenproof baking dish, and bake, uncovered, at 425° for 35–45 minutes or until the sauce is bubbly and the potatoes are tender. Makes approximately 4–6 servings.

Photo Courtesy of Nancy Feldbush

Chef's Comments

Herbs de Provence can be purchased at most specialty stores or online at www.AllThingsLavender.com.

You can also create your own Herbs de Provence by following the recipe on page 19.

Recipe Tested in the Kitchen of Nancy Feldbush

Lavender Lane

Lunch Favorites

Spinach Pie with Lavender Feta Cheese

There are many variations of spinach pie, but my adaptation of an authentic Greek recipe happens to be my favorite. The lavender and feta cheese offer a nice complement to the onions, garlic, carrots, and spinach. And, as if that couldn't get any better, the entire pie is wrapped between crispy, flaky layers of phyllo dough. It's a meal all in itself and tastes even better the next day.

3 bags (10 oz. size) baby spinach leaves, washed

1 cup whole milk (do not use any substitutions)

2 large eggs, slightly beaten

2 large egg yolks, slightly beaten

3 garlic cloves, minced

1/2 cup yellow sweet onion, finely minced

1/2 cup carrots, peeled and finely minced

1/2 cup fresh parsley, chopped

1 tsp sea salt

1 tsp fresh-ground black pepper

1/2 cup ricotta cheese

1/2 tsp Organic Culinary Lavender Buds

1 cup feta cheese

8 sheets phyllo dough

olive oil (for brushing)

Preheat the oven to 350°F. Lightly oil a 9-inch square baking dish with olive oil. Place the spinach in a large pot of boiling water, and cook for 2 minutes.

Drain, and allow to cool for 5 minutes. Wrap the spinach in a clean kitchen towel, and squeeze out as much of the water as possible. Finely chop the spinach, and set aside.

In a large mixing bowl, whisk together the milk, eggs, egg yolks, garlic, onion, carrots, parsley, salt, and pepper. Add the spinach, ricotta cheese, lavender buds, and feta cheese, and mix well.

Lay 1 sheet of the phyllo dough in the prepared baking dish, and brush lightly with olive oil. Lay another sheet of phyllo dough on top of the previous sheet, and brush with olive oil. Repeat this step 2 more times until you have 4 layers of the phyllo dough on the bottom of the baking dish. The sheets will overlap the pan, which is fine.

Spoon the spinach and cheese mixture into the pan. Top the spinach with a sheet of phyllo dough. Brush the phyllo dough with oil, and then layer the remaining 3 sheets of phyllo dough on top, brushing with oil each time. Tuck any overhanging dough into the sides of the pan to seal the filling. Bake, uncovered, at 350° for 35–40 minutes or until golden brown. Cut into squares, and serve while hot. Makes approximately 6–8 servings.

Photo Courtesy of Maureen Buecking

Recipe Tested in the Kitchen of Maureen Buecking

Basil & Lavender Pesto Rustic Pizza

Homemade pesto and sun-dried tomatoes create a heavenly duo in this delightful pizza. Any variety of prepared pizza crust can be used, but we prefer a Boboli ready-made crust, which can be found near the dairy section at most supermarkets.

Basil & Lavender Pesto (see the recipe on the next page)

1 large Boboli ready-made pizza crust (or 4 small)

4 Roma tomatoes, seeded and thinly sliced

10 baby spinach leaves, thinly sliced

1/2 yellow bell pepper, thinly sliced

1/4 cup black olives, sliced

1 1/2 cups shredded Italian cheese blend
(we prefer Kraft brand) OR feta cheese

1/4 cup fresh-grated Parmesan cheese

> ## Chef's Comments
>
> *When using fresh tomatoes on a pizza, be sure to remove the seeds and juices first; otherwise, they will make the pizza soggy.*

Preheat the oven to 450°F.

Spread the Basil & Lavender Pesto over the Boboli crust. Place the tomatoes, spinach, yellow pepper, and black olives onto the pizza, distributing them evenly. Top with the cheeses.

Bake at 450° on a foil-lined cookie sheet for 10 minutes or until the cheeses melt. Allow the pizza to cool for 2 minutes before cutting. Cut into slices, and serve warm. Makes approximately 6 servings.

Basil & Lavender Pesto

2 Tbsp sun-dried tomatoes

1/2 cup fresh basil

1/2 tsp Organic Culinary Lavender
    Buds

1 tsp fresh parsley

2 Tbsp pine nuts

1/4 tsp red pepper flakes

2 garlic cloves, minced

2 Tbsp fresh-grated Parmesan
    cheese

2 Tbsp Romano cheese, shredded

1/8 tsp salt

3 Tbsp olive oil

Fill a small saucepan with water, and bring it to a boil. Remove the pan
from the heat, and place the sun-dried tomatoes into the water for about
10 minutes to allow them to plump up. Drain the sun-dried tomatoes,
and put them on a paper towel to absorb any extra water. Combine all
the ingredients, except for the olive oil, in a blender or food processor,
and pulse until well blended, scraping the sides with a spatula as needed.
Gradually add the olive oil while the machine is running, and mix well.

Photo Courtesy of Debbie Walter

Recipe Tested in the Kitchen of Debbie Walter

Lavender, Black Bean & Beef Quesadillas

These quesadillas are full of flavor and pizzazz and make a quick yet filling lunch. You can use any variety of meat in the filling, and I sometimes toss in a sliced avocado for a yummy change of pace.

1 tsp olive oil

1/2 small yellow onion, finely diced

1/2 pound ground round

1/2 tsp Organic Culinary Lavender Buds

1/4 tsp chili powder

garlic salt (to taste)

fresh-ground black pepper (to taste)

1 can (15 oz. size) black beans, drained

1 cup salsa

8 large flour tortillas

1 1/2 cups shredded Mexican cheese blend

Preheat the oven to 400°F.

In a large skillet, heat the olive oil over medium heat, and then add the onion. Stir well until the onion is coated with the olive oil. Add the ground round, lavender buds, chili powder, garlic salt, and pepper. Stir while cooking to break up any large chunks of ground round as you brown the meat. Cook until the meat is no longer pink, about 5–7 minutes.

Remove from the heat, and drain the oil from the ground round. Return the meat to the stove, add the black beans and salsa, and continue to cook while mashing the beans in with the meat.

Arrange 4 of the tortillas on a well-greased cookie sheet. Spread the meat filling evenly among the tortillas, and sprinkle the cheese evenly over each. Lay a tortilla on top of each quesadilla, and press down lightly.

Bake at 400° for 8 minutes or until golden brown. Cut each quesadilla into 4 wedges. Makes approximately 4 servings.

Chef's Comments

For a unique taste sensation, try using my Mango Lavender Salsa in this recipe. The different flavors blend together beautifully. Mango Lavender Salsa can be found on page 148.

Recipe Tested in the Kitchen of Valerie Harms

Pasta Primavera with Lavender Red Wine Vinaigrette

This sensational pasta salad is made with grilled vegetables and is equally delicious when served warm or cold. Fresh, seasonal vegetables can easily be substituted for any of the ones listed here, making the variations of this recipe endless.

2 carrots, peeled and cut into thin strips

1 yellow bell pepper, cut into thin strips

1 small zucchini, cut into thin strips

1 yellow squash, cut into thin strips

1 small onion, thinly sliced

1/4 cup olive oil

salt (to taste)

fresh-ground black pepper (to taste)

Photo Courtesy of Kim Parr

1 pound uncooked bow tie pasta (this type of pasta is also called farfalle)

1/2 pint cherry tomatoes, cut in half

1/2 cup sliced black olives

Lavender Red Wine Vinaigrette (see the recipe on the next page)

1/2 cup fresh-grated Parmesan cheese

Preheat the oven to 450°F. In a large mixing bowl, toss together the carrots, bell pepper, zucchini, squash, and onion with the oil. Season with a touch of salt and pepper, to taste. Arrange the vegetables on a large, foil-lined baking sheet, spreading them out evenly. Bake at 450° for about 10 minutes, and then turn the vegetables over. Continue to bake for approximately 10 more minutes or until the carrots are tender and the vegetables begin to brown.

While the vegetables are baking, prepare the pasta. Cook the pasta in a pot of boiling water for about 8 minutes or until "al dente" (tender but still firm to the bite). Drain the pasta, and set aside.

In a large bowl, toss the pasta together with the grilled vegetables. Add the tomatoes and black olives, and mix well. Prepare the Lavender Red Wine Vinaigrette, and then drizzle just enough of the dressing over the pasta to moisten the ingredients. Mix well, and add more dressing, to taste, if needed. Sprinkle with the fresh-grated Parmesan cheese, and serve immediately. Makes approximately 6–8 servings.

Lavender Red Wine Vinaigrette

1/2 cup red wine vinegar

4 Tbsp fresh-squeezed lemon juice

1 Tbsp honey

1 tsp salt

1/2 tsp fresh-ground black pepper

1/2 tsp Organic Culinary Lavender
Buds

3/4 cup extra-virgin olive oil

In a blender or food processor, mix together the vinegar, lemon juice, honey, salt, pepper, and lavender buds. Pulse a few times until the ingredients are mixed. With the machine running, gradually add the olive oil, a little at a time. Refrigerate any unused vinaigrette for up to 1 week. This dressing also tastes fabulous on any garden salad.

Recipe Tested in the Kitchen of Kim Parr

Herb Garden Pasta

During the peak of harvest time, summer gardens and local farm markets are full of fresh herbs. This salad celebrates the richness of those herbs, and the tomatoes and goat cheese add a flavorful touch. The predominant flavors in this salad are basil and rosemary, and lavender complements their taste without being overpowering.

1/2 pound (8 oz.) uncooked penne pasta

1 1/2 tsp extra-virgin olive oil, plus 1 1/2 tsp, separated

1/4 cup fresh basil, chopped

2 Tbsp fresh parsley, chopped

1/2 tsp Organic Culinary Lavender Buds, chopped

1/4 tsp sea salt

1/4 tsp fresh-ground black pepper

1 garlic clove, minced

1/2 red onion, minced

2 tsp fresh chives, chopped

2 tsp fresh rosemary, chopped

1 pint cherry tomatoes

3 Tbsp vegetable broth

2 Tbsp butter

1/3 cup goat cheese, crumbled

a fresh sprig of basil (for garnish—optional)

Cook the pasta according to the package's directions, and drain. Place the pasta in a large bowl, and toss with 1 1/2 tsp of olive oil. Add the basil, parsley, lavender buds, salt, and pepper, and toss well to combine.

In a large skillet, mix together the remaining 1 1/2 tsp of olive oil, garlic, onion, chives, and rosemary. Sauté the ingredients over medium-low heat for 4 minutes, stirring frequently. Add the tomatoes, and continue sautéing until the skins of the tomatoes are slightly charred and just beginning to burst.

Add the vegetable broth and butter, and bring to a boil. Cover, and cook for 1 minute. Remove from the heat, and add the tomato and onion mixture to the pasta. Toss well to combine. Sprinkle with the goat cheese, and garnish with a fresh sprig of basil, if desired. Serve immediately. Makes approximately 2–4 servings.

Photo Courtesy of Tony Kampling

Recipe Tested in the Kitchen of Tony Kampling

Lavender Couscous Chicken Bowl

Couscous...is it a pasta or a grain or something else? Sources differ on the definition, but they all agree that couscous, a North African staple, is made from semolina flour, which is also an ingredient in pasta. My family loves it in this dish because it offers a unique texture. The flavors of chicken, couscous, vegetables, and lavender blend together so well—this admirable lunch recipe is sure to become a fast favorite.

1 can (14 oz. size) low-sodium chicken broth

1 1/4 cups quick-cooking couscous

1 pkg (6 oz. size) precooked chicken breast strips, cut into chunks

1 cup preshredded broccoli slaw

1 cup carrots, shredded

1 cup cherry tomatoes, halved

Dressing

3 Tbsp apple cider vinegar

2 Tbsp extra-virgin olive oil

2 Tbsp fresh-squeezed lemon juice

1 Tbsp granulated sugar

2 tsp Lavender Lemon Pepper (see the recipe on page 18)

1–2 garlic cloves, finely minced (to taste)

salt (to taste)

fresh-ground black pepper (to taste)

Chef's Comments

Broccoli slaw, or shredded broccoli, can be found in the produce section at most grocery stores.

In a medium-size saucepan, heat the chicken broth over medium-high heat until it comes to a boil. Stir in the couscous, cover, and remove from the heat. Let it stand for 5 minutes to absorb the broth, and then fluff with a fork.

In a large bowl, combine together the chicken, broccoli slaw, carrots, and tomatoes, and mix well. Add the couscous, and toss the ingredients together. Set aside.

To make the Dressing, in a small bowl, whisk together the vinegar, olive oil, lemon juice, sugar, Lavender Lemon Pepper, and 1–2 garlic cloves, depending on your garlic taste preference. Continue to whisk vigorously until all of the ingredients are well incorporated.

Drizzle the Dressing over the other ingredients, and toss to coat. Season, to taste, with the salt and pepper, if desired. Serve in individual bowls. Makes approximately 2–4 servings.

Photo Courtesy of Tony Kampling

Recipe Tested in the Kitchen of Tony Kampling

Lavender & Lime Infused Fruit Salad

On those steamy summer days, when it is just too hot to turn on the stove, try this simple and scrumptious fruit salad. The Lavender Sugar blends beautifully with the lime, giving the fruit a delicate flavor boost.

1 medium cantaloupe, cut into 1/2-inch chunks

1 medium honeydew melon, cut into 1/2-inch chunks

2 peaches, pitted and sliced

1 pint strawberries, sliced in half

1 pint fresh berries (blueberries OR blackberries)

2 cups seedless grapes (red OR green)

4 limes, juiced

3 Tbsp Lavender Sugar (see the recipe on the next page)

1/3 cup sliced almonds

Place all of the fruit in a large salad bowl, and toss with the fresh-squeezed lime juice. Sprinkle with the Lavender Sugar, and toss well to coat all the fruit pieces. Garnish with sliced almonds, and serve. Makes approximately 10–12 servings.

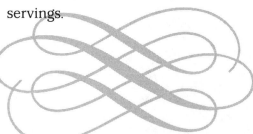

Lavender Sugar

2 cups granulated sugar
4 Tbsp Organic Culinary Lavender Buds

Mix together the sugar and lavender buds, and place in a covered container. Store at room temperature for 1–2 weeks, shaking the container occasionally to distribute the lavender among the sugar granules. Pass the sugar through a strainer to remove the buds, and store the Lavender Sugar in an airtight container. For a more profound lavender taste, crush the lavender buds in a spice grinder or coffee grinder before mixing with the sugar, and do not remove them from the sugar.

Photo Courtesy of Heidi Bitsoli

Recipe Tested in the Bitsoli Kitchen

Smoked Cheddar & Beef with Lavender Horseradish Cream

A classic beef and cheddar sandwich is not complete without a creamy horseradish dressing. You'll be pleasantly surprised by the subtle goodness that lavender lends to this already legendary sandwich.

4 French bread rolls (2 oz. size)

8 oz. thinly sliced roast beef

4 slices (1 oz. each) smoked cheddar cheese

1/2 red onion, thinly sliced

1 large tomato, thinly sliced

2 romaine lettuce leaves, cut in half

Lavender Horseradish Cream (see the recipe on the next page)

Preheat the oven to 475°F. Cut the French bread rolls horizontally, and place the bottom half on a cookie sheet. Evenly divide the roast beef and cheese among the rolls, placing the cheese on top. Bake at 475° for 4–5 minutes or until the cheese is melted.

Remove from the oven, and evenly divide the onion, tomato slices, and lettuce leaves among the sandwiches, laying them over the beef and cheese. Spread, to taste, the Lavender Horseradish Cream over the top half of the rolls, and place them on top of the sandwiches. Makes 4 servings.

Lavender Horseradish Cream

1/2 cup sour cream

1 Tbsp white horseradish

1/2 tsp Organic Culinary Lavender Buds

salt (to taste)

fresh-ground black pepper (to taste)

In a small bowl, mix together the sour cream, horseradish, and lavender buds until well incorporated. Add the salt and pepper, to taste. Unused horseradish cream may be refrigerated in a covered container for up to 2 days.

Photo Courtesy of Tony Kampling

Recipe Tested in the Kitchen of Tony Kampling

Mediterranean Lavender Grilled Veggie Pita

This lunch is absolutely delicious and quite satisfying. The vegetables can be marinated a day or two ahead, cutting the preparation time in half. The grilled vegetables also make a wonderful side dish—just eliminate the pita bread, and serve the veggies alongside your favorite main dish, such as grilled steak or seafood.

1 red bell pepper, seeded and cored

1 green bell pepper, seeded and cored

1 pkg (8 oz. size) portobello mushrooms

1/2 red onion

1 small zucchini OR yellow squash

Mediterranean Lavender Marinade (see the
    recipe on the next page)

6 pieces Greek flat bread OR pita bread

1/2 cup feta cheese

2 cups cherry tomatoes, cut in half

1/3 cup fresh cilantro leaves

Photo Courtesy of Linda Mascagni

Cut the bell peppers, mushrooms, and onion into slices, about 1 1/2–2 inches wide. Cut the zucchini or squash into 1/2-inch-thick slices. Place the sliced vegetables in a large mixing bowl. Pour the Mediterranean Lavender Marinade over the sliced vegetables, and toss until the veggies are well coated. Cover, refrigerate, and allow the vegetables to marinate for at least 2 hours or overnight before grilling.

Preheat the oven to 150°F. Wrap the flat bread or pita bread in foil, and place them in the oven to warm them just before you grill the vegetables.

Prepare an outdoor barbecue grill for direct cooking, or heat up an indoor grill, such as a George Foreman grill, panini grill, or stove-top griddle. Remove the vegetables from the marinade, and place them on the grill. Keep the marinade to use later. Grill the veggies until they are blackened. If using an outdoor barbecue grill or a stove-top griddle, turn over the vegetables once to blacken both sides. Remove the vegetables from the grill when they are done, drizzle the reserved marinade over them, and cover to keep them warm.

Remove the bread from the oven, and place the vegetables, dividing them evenly, on top of the bread. Sprinkle with the feta cheese, cherry tomatoes, and cilantro leaves. Wrap the bread around the veggies, and serve immediately. Makes approximately 6 servings.

Mediterranean Lavender Marinade

1/4 cup fresh-squeezed lime juice

2 Tbsp extra-virgin olive oil

1/8 tsp fresh-ground black pepper

1/8 tsp sea salt

1/2 tsp Organic Culinary Lavender Buds

1/8 tsp dried mint leaves

1 garlic clove, minced

Combine together all of the ingredients in a small mixing bowl, and whisk until smooth.

Recipe Tested in the Kitchen of Linda Mascagni

Traverse City Cherry & Turkey Wrap with Lavender Raspberry Vinaigrette

Traverse City, Michigan, is well known for many things—including the National Cherry Festival, which is held annually in July. And cherries from Traverse City are featured in many different recipes, including variations of this sandwich, throughout the Great Lakes State. I like to use my homemade Lavender Raspberry Vinaigrette when making these wraps at home. It adds a purely delectable flavor to this already scrumptious sandwich.

4 whole wheat tortillas

12 slices roasted turkey breast

12 thin slices of cucumber

1/2 cup dried cherries

1/4 cup pecans, finely chopped

1 cup mixed greens

1/4 red onion, thinly sliced

1/3 cup blue cheese (optional)

Lavender Raspberry Vinaigrette (see the recipe on the next page)

Divide the ingredients, except the vinaigrette, evenly between the 4 tortillas, layering each ingredient on top of the other on half of the tortilla. Drizzle the Lavender Raspberry Vinaigrette, to taste, over the filling.

Beginning with the side that is layered with the ingredients, firmly roll up the tortilla from one end to the other. Cut the wrap in half, and place a toothpick in the center of each half. Serve with a dill pickle and baked potato crisps for a great lunchtime meal. Makes 4 servings.

Lavender Raspberry Vinaigrette

1/2 cup raspberries, fresh OR
    frozen
1/4 cup balsamic vinegar
1/4 cup white wine vinegar
2 tsp granulated sugar

1 Tbsp Dijon mustard
2 tsp Organic Culinary Lavender
    Buds
1/2 cup extra-virgin olive oil

Combine all of the ingredients, except for the oil, in a blender or food processor, and mix well. While mixing, slowly add the oil, a little at a time, until the dressing thickens and is well blended. This dressing is thicker than most vinaigrettes; if preferred, it can be thinned by simply adding more oil and vinegar to taste.

Photo Courtesy of Debbie Walter

Recipe Tested in the Kitchen of Debbie Walter

Lavender Roasted Chicken Waldorf Salad Croissants

If you remember your grandmother mixing together a Waldorf salad, raise your hand. My sandwich version keeps all the memories but adds chicken and lavender, which jazzes up the old classic a bit—I think our grandmothers would be pleasantly surprised.

1 Tbsp olive oil

2 boneless, skinless chicken breasts

1/2 fresh lemon

2 tsp Organic Culinary Lavender Buds

salt (to taste)

fresh-ground black pepper (to taste)

2 stalks celery, chopped

1 Granny Smith apple, peeled, cored, and chopped

1 cup seedless red grapes, cut in half

1/2 cup walnuts, chopped

1/2 cup light mayonnaise

4 croissants, sliced in half

4 romaine lettuce leaves

In a medium-size frying pan, heat the olive oil over medium heat, and add the chicken to the pan. Squeeze the juice from the 1/2 lemon over the chicken. Sprinkle the lavender buds, salt, and pepper over the chicken. Cover, reduce the heat to low, and sauté for about 7 minutes. Turn the chicken over, and continue to sauté until the chicken is completely cooked, about 14–18 minutes total. Remove from the heat, and allow the chicken to cool. Cut the chicken into small cubes when it cools to room temperature.

In a medium-size bowl, combine the chicken, celery, apple, grapes, walnuts, and mayonnaise. Mix well. Separate the two halves of the croissants, and place a lettuce leaf on each bottom half. Divide the salad evenly among the 4 sandwiches, and cover with the top halves of the croissants. Makes 4 servings.

Photo Courtesy of Debbie Walter

Recipe Tested in the Kitchen of Debbie Walter

Turkey Focaccia Sandwich with Lavender Chipotle Mayo

The flavor of this sandwich is best described as outstanding. The Lavender Chipotle Mayo is easy to make, adds a little heat, and tastes sensational on this sandwich!

1 loaf (10 oz. size) focaccia bread

Lavender Chipotle Mayo (see the recipe
on the next page)

2 1/2 cups honey-roasted turkey
breast, shredded

1 garden-fresh tomato, thinly sliced

2 Tbsp fresh basil, chopped

1/4 red onion, thinly sliced

1/2 cup mozzarella cheese

1 tsp olive oil

Photo Courtesy of Maureen Buecking

Slice the focaccia bread in half horizontally. Spread 2 Tbsp of Lavender Chipotle Mayo on the bottom half of the bread. Evenly arrange the turkey breast over the top of the mayo. Layer the tomato slices, basil, and onion evenly over the turkey. Sprinkle with the cheese. Spread 2 Tbsp of Lavender Chipotle Mayo on the top half of the bread, and place it on top of the sandwich. Press gently.

Heat a large nonstick skillet over medium heat, and add the 1 tsp olive oil. Add the sandwich to the pan, and place a cast-iron or heavy skillet on top of the sandwich, pressing down gently to flatten it. Cook for 2 minutes or until the bread is lightly toasted, leaving the cast-iron skillet on top of the sandwich while it is toasting in the pan. Turn the sandwich over, and repeat. Cut into 4 wedges, and serve with your favorite pasta salad or fresh fruit. Makes approximately 4–6 servings.

Lavender Chipotle Mayo

1/2 cup light mayonnaise (do not use any substitutions)

1 chipotle chili in adobo sauce, plus 1 tsp of the adobo sauce

1 tsp Organic Culinary Lavender Buds

1 garlic clove, peeled

1 Tbsp fresh-squeezed lime juice

In a food processor or blender, combine together all of the ingredients. Pulse to mix, scraping down the sides of the bowl as needed. Pulse 8–12 times or until well blended.

Chef's Comments

Chipotle chilies in adobo sauce can be found in the international aisle at most supermarkets. They usually come in bottles; although sometimes, they are canned.

If you like it hot, try adding an extra chipotle chili to the mayo along with an extra teaspoon of the adobo sauce.

Lavender Chipotle Mayo also tastes great on everything from burgers and BLTs to veggies and tortilla chips!

Recipe Tested in the Kitchen of Maureen Buecking

Lavender Lane

Appetizers, Vegetables & Sides

Garlic & Herb Cream Cheese Dip

This dip can be easily whipped up whenever a yummy appetizer is needed because many of the ingredients are already on the pantry shelves or in the spice rack. I've also lowered the fat content—without losing any of the flavor—so dive in, and enjoy.

1 pkg (8 oz. size) fat-free cream cheese

1/4 cup fat-free sour cream

1/4 cup fresh-grated Parmesan cheese

1/4 cup red bell pepper, finely minced

1 Tbsp dehydrated garlic

1 Tbsp dehydrated onion

2 tsp dried basil

1 tsp Organic Culinary Lavender Buds, chopped

1 tsp dried chives

1 tsp dried parsley

1/4 tsp sea salt

Dash of fresh-ground black pepper

In a small mixing bowl, beat together the cream cheese, sour cream, and Parmesan cheese with an electric mixer until smooth. Add the remaining ingredients, and blend well. Refrigerate the dip overnight before serving to allow the flavors to mature. Makes approximately 8 servings.

Variation

For a fancy presentation, serve the dip in a hollowed-out red bell pepper. Place the pepper in the middle of a decorative plate, and surround it with fresh vegetables and crackers for dipping.

Chef's Comments

To save time, premix several batches of the dried herbs, and store them in individual containers. The herbs will keep for quite a while, and they'll be ready—and premeasured—for making a batch of the dip anytime.

This dip is definitely for garlic lovers! If you prefer a more mellow garlic flavor, reduce the amount of garlic in the recipe to 1 tsp.

Photo Courtesy of Julie Kampling

Recipe Tested in the Kitchen of Julie Kampling

Hot Spinach Lavender Artichoke Dip

Always a big hit at gatherings, this dip is at its best when served with tortilla chips. To spice things up—and depending on how hot you want your dip to be—add some minced jalapeño peppers just before baking.

2 Tbsp butter

1/4 cup yellow onion, minced

2 garlic cloves, minced

1/4 cup carrots, finely shredded

1 pkg (8 oz. size) cream cheese, softened

1/2 cup mayonnaise

1/2 cup sour cream

1/2 tsp fresh-ground black pepper

1 tsp Organic Culinary Lavender Buds

2 tsp fresh-squeezed lemon juice

1 pkg (10 oz. size) frozen chopped spinach, thawed and squeezed dry

1/4 cup fresh-grated Parmesan cheese, plus 1/4 cup, separated

1 cup shredded Italian cheese blend (we prefer Kraft brand)

1 can (8 oz. size) water chestnuts, drained and chopped

1 can (14 oz. size) marinated artichoke hearts, drained and chopped

Preheat the oven to 350°F. In medium-size saucepan, heat the butter over low heat, and sauté the onion, garlic, and carrots until the onion is tender, about 5 minutes. Remove from the heat, and set aside.

In a large mixing bowl, beat together the cream cheese, mayonnaise, and sour cream with an electric mixer on medium speed until smooth.

Add the pepper, lavender buds, and lemon juice, and beat well. Add the onion and garlic mixture, along with the spinach, 1/4 cup of Parmesan cheese, cheese blend, water chestnuts, and artichoke hearts. Mix thoroughly using just a large spoon.

Transfer the dip to a 2-quart casserole dish, and sprinkle with the remaining 1/4 cup of Parmesan cheese. Bake at 350° for 15–20 minutes or until lightly browned on top. Serve with tortilla chips, Wheat Thins, or your favorite crackers. Makes approximately 3 1/2 cups.

Chef's Comments

You can easily control the fat content of this dip. Just choose low-fat variations of the cream cheese, mayonnaise, sour cream, and Italian cheese blend for a light appetizer. Or make the recipe using "regular" versions of those ingredients for a richer dip.

Recipe Tested in the Kitchen of Arlene Hicks

Lavender & Parmesan "Oven Fried" Zucchini

For a quick and easy appetizer that tastes amazing, you've got to try this! The oven method makes these zucchini chips crisp and tasty, and you can feel good about eating them because they are so much lower in fat than their "fried" counterparts. My family and I like them served with Lavender Buttermilk Ranch Dressing, which can be found on page 168, but cocktail sauce also makes a good companion for this savory snack.

3 medium zucchini

1/3 cup egg substitute (we prefer Egg Beaters brand)

1/2 cup Italian-style bread crumbs

1/2 tsp Organic Culinary Lavender Buds, ground

1/8 tsp garlic powder

1/4 cup fresh-grated Parmesan cheese

1/8 tsp fresh-ground black pepper

dash of salt

Preheat the oven to 475°F. Spray a cookie sheet with nonstick cooking spray, and set aside. Cut the zucchini into 1/4-inch-thick slices, and set aside.

Place the egg substitute into a small bowl. In a separate bowl, combine together the bread crumbs, ground lavender buds, garlic powder, Parmesan cheese, pepper, and salt. Stir until all ingredients are well blended.

Dip the zucchini slices into the egg substitute, and then transfer them to the bowl with the bread crumb mixture. Turn the zucchini over until well coated.

Place the seasoned zucchini slices on the prepared cookie sheet, spreading them out evenly.

Bake the zucchini at 475° for 5 minutes. Turn the slices over, and bake for an additional 5 minutes or until they are golden brown. Serve immediately. Makes approximately 4–6 hors d'oeuvre-size servings.

Chef's Comments

If you would rather use regular eggs instead of the egg substitute, just beat 2 eggs until they are very smooth and frothy.

Photo Courtesy of Kim Parr

Recipe Tested in the Kitchen of Kim Parr

Heirloom Tomatoes & Cucumbers with Lavender Lime Marinade

*There's nothing quite like just-picked, homegrown, fresh-from-the-garden
tomatoes and cucumbers. I have a fondness for heirloom varieties because
I believe their taste is second to none—but feel free to use your favorites.
When combined with the tanginess of lime and the sweetness of lavender, the
natural goodness of these two wonderful vegetables comes alive!*

1 pound assorted ripe tomatoes, cut into bite-size wedges

1 English cucumber, cut into bite-size wedges

1/3 cup Lavender Lime Marinade (see the recipe on the next page)

Decoratively arrange the tomato and cucumber wedges in a serving bowl, and
drizzle the Lavender Lime Marinade over the vegetables. Cover, and refrigerate
for at least 2 hours before serving. Makes approximately 8 servings.

Lavender Lime Marinade

1/2 cup fresh-squeezed lime juice

2 Tbsp granulated sugar

2 tsp Organic Culinary Lavender Buds

1/4 tsp garlic salt

1/4 tsp fresh-ground black pepper

1 cup extra-virgin olive oil

In a small mixing bowl, combine the lime juice, sugar, lavender buds, garlic salt, and pepper. With an electric mixer, beat the mixture on low speed while slowly adding the olive oil. Store the marinade in a covered container in the refrigerator for up to 2 weeks.

Photo Courtesy of Debbie Walter

Recipe Tested in the Kitchen of Debbie Walter

Herbs de Provence Stuffed Tomatoes

Both an easy and elegant side dish, these stuffed tomatoes overflow with aromatic flavor, healthful goodness, and wonderful color. They can also become the center of a filling vegetarian meal by surrounding them with steamed vegetables and a hearty, whole-grain bread.

Stuffing

1 cup uncooked Uncle Ben's long grain and wild rice

4 Tbsp butter

1/3 cup onion, finely diced

2 cloves garlic, minced

1/2 cup carrots, finely shredded

1 cup baby spinach leaves, thinly sliced (about 18–20 leaves)

1 1/2 tsp Herbs de Provence (with lavender)

1/3 cup dry bread crumbs

1 cup feta cheese

1/3 cup fresh-grated Parmesan cheese

Tomatoes

1 Tbsp olive oil

6 medium-large tomatoes (ripe but firm)

salt (to taste)

fresh-ground black pepper (to taste)

Topping

2 Tbsp olive oil

2 Tbsp bread crumbs

2 Tbsp fresh-grated Parmesan cheese

1 Tbsp dried parsley

Chef's Comments

We prefer to use beefsteak, heirloom, or yellow tomatoes for this recipe. Other medium-large tomatoes may be substituted, but don't use cherry or grape tomatoes since they will be too small.

To easily slice the spinach, stack up 4–5 leaves, then firmly roll them together before slicing. This will give you nice thin strips.

To make the stuffing, cook the rice, according to the package's directions, in a medium saucepan. Rinse the rice under cold running water, drain, and set aside.

In a large skillet, heat the butter over medium-low heat, and sauté the onion, garlic, and carrots for 4 minutes, stirring often. Add the spinach, reduce the heat to low, and continue sautéing for another 4 minutes. Remove the mixture from the heat, and add the remaining ingredients for the stuffing. Mix well, and set aside.

Preheat the oven to 350°F. Lightly oil a baking dish with 1 Tbsp of olive oil. Cut the tops off the tomatoes. Scoop out and discard the seeds. Slice a very thin piece off the bottom of each tomato—this will keep them from toppling over while baking. Lightly season the inside of the tomatoes with salt and pepper, to taste.

Spoon the stuffing into the tomatoes, mounding slightly, and place them in the baking dish. Place any leftover stuffing on the bottom of the pan around the tomatoes. To create the Topping, drizzle the tomatoes with 2 Tbsp of olive oil, and then sprinkle them with the remaining Topping ingredients. Bake at 350°, uncovered, for 20–25 minutes or until heated through. For a nice golden brown top, place the tomatoes under the broiler for 2 minutes, watching them carefully so they don't burn. The tomatoes may be served hot or cooled to room temperature. Makes 6 servings.

Chef's Comments

Herbs de Provence can be purchased at most specialty stores or online at www.AllThingsLavender.com.

You can also create your own Herbs de Provence by following the recipe on page 19.

Recipe Tested in the Kitchen of Diane Dueweke

Lavender, Asiago & Spinach Stuffed Mushrooms

Filled with fresh asiago cheese, green onion, lavender, and spinach, these flavorful mushroom caps make a side dish or appetizer that will dress up even the simplest of foods. For brunch, keep the mushrooms on a warming tray, and serve with an array of breakfast cheeses, muffins, and fresh fruits.

1 Tbsp olive oil

18 mushrooms (1 1/2–2 inches in diameter)

1/4 tsp Organic Culinary Lavender Buds

4 Tbsp butter, melted

2 Tbsp bread crumbs

1 pkg (12 oz. size) Stouffer's brand frozen spinach soufflé, thawed

2 Tbsp green onion, finely diced

1/3 cup asiago cheese, grated

2–3 Tbsp fresh-grated Parmesan cheese (for garnish)

Preheat the oven to 400°F. Lightly oil a 9-inch square baking dish with the 1 Tbsp of olive oil.

Wash the mushrooms, and carefully remove the stems. Place the mushroom caps in the baking dish, hollow side up, keeping them slightly apart.

In a spice grinder or coffee grinder, chop the lavender buds until finely ground, and set aside.

In a small mixing bowl, combine together the melted butter, bread crumbs, spinach, onion, and asiago cheese, along with the ground lavender buds. Mix well.

Evenly fill the mushrooms with the mixture. Sprinkle with the fresh-grated Parmesan cheese, and bake at 400°F for 20 minutes. Serve hot. Makes approximately 6–8 servings.

Recipe Tested in the Kitchen of Arlene Hicks

Spiced Lavender Honey-Glazed Carrots with Apples

These savory and sweet carrots will transform even the staunchest vegetable-skeptic into a vegetable-admirer.

6 large carrots, sliced

4 large apples, peeled, cored, and sliced (Cortland, Gala, or Golden Delicious apples work the best)

1/4 cup all-purpose flour

1/4 cup packed brown sugar

1/4 tsp nutmeg

1/4 tsp cinnamon

1/2 tsp Organic Culinary Lavender Buds

1 Tbsp butter

1/4 cup honey

1/2 cup orange juice

1/4 cup pecans, chopped (optional)

Preheat the oven to 350°F. Place the carrots in a large saucepan, and cover with water. Bring the carrots to a boil, and cook for 5 minutes. Drain the carrots, and set aside.

In a large casserole dish, layer the apples and carrots in a decorative fashion. Combine the flour, sugar, nutmeg, cinnamon, and lavender buds in a small mixing bowl, and stir well. Sprinkle the flour and spices over the apples and carrots.

In a small saucepan, melt together the butter, honey, and orange juice, stirring occasionally. Once the ingredients are melted and well mixed, drizzle over the flour mixture. Sprinkle with the chopped pecans, if desired, and bake at 350° for 30 minutes or until the carrots are tender. Makes approximately 8–10 servings.

Photo Courtesy of Debbie Walter

Recipe Tested in the Kitchen of Debbie Walter

Lavender Parmesan Baked Asparagus

Many people will shy away from asparagus because it isn't as commonly seen as peas and carrots. But this vegetable is absolutely wonderful when baked with a bit of olive oil and seasoned with lavender. Even if you've never tried asparagus before, my quick-and-easy Lavender Parmesan Baked Asparagus will turn this vegetable into an instant favorite.

1 pound fresh asparagus spears
1 Tbsp olive oil, plus 1 Tbsp, separated
1/4 tsp Organic Culinary Lavender Buds
sea salt (to taste)
fresh-ground black pepper (to taste)
1/4 cup fresh-grated Parmesan cheese
1/4 cup Romano cheese, shredded

Preheat the oven to 400°F.

Trim off the woody bottoms of the asparagus, and then wash and drain the spears. Place the asparagus in a large, shallow baking dish, and drizzle 1 Tbsp of olive oil over the spears, stirring until the vegetable is evenly coated with the oil.

Place the asparagus in a single layer on a cookie sheet, and drizzle the remaining 1 Tbsp of olive oil over the top. Sprinkle on the lavender buds, salt, and pepper, and bake at 400° until tender, about 10–15 minutes.

Remove the spears from the oven, and top with the cheeses. Serve immediately. Makes approximately 3–4 servings.

Chef's Comments

If you prefer a crunchier asparagus, increase the cooking time to 18–20 minutes.

Photo Courtesy of Bonnie Feldbush

Recipe Tested in the Kitchen of Bonnie Feldbush

Green Beans Almondine with Lavender Dill Butter

This savory side dish goes with just about any meal, and the Lavender Dill Butter enhances the flavor of an already great twosome: green beans and almonds.

1/3 cup sliced almonds
1 pkg (9 oz. size) frozen cut Italian green beans
4 Tbsp Lavender Dill Butter (see the recipe on the next page)
1/2 tsp sea salt
fresh-ground black pepper (to taste)

Place the sliced almonds in a large skillet, and toast them over medium-low heat, tossing frequently, until golden brown. Remove the almonds from the skillet, and set aside.

In a medium-size soup pot, bring 2 quarts of water to a boil. Cook the green beans in the boiling water for 5 minutes. Drain the beans, and place them in ice-cold water to "shock" them, which will keep their color bright green.

In the skillet, melt the Lavender Dill Butter, and then add the sea salt and pepper. Mix well. Add the green beans, and stir them in the Lavender Dill Butter until they are heated through and evenly coated. Sprinkle with the toasted almonds, and serve immediately. Makes approximately 4 servings.

Photo Courtesy of Julie Kampling

Lavender Dill Butter

2 Tbsp fresh dill, finely chopped

1 Tbsp Organic Culinary Lavender Buds, finely chopped

2 sticks butter, softened

2 garlic cloves, minced

1 tsp fresh-squeezed lemon juice

Place the finely chopped dill and lavender buds in a large mixing bowl. Add the remaining ingredients, and with an electric mixer, blend on low speed until smooth and creamy. Shape the butter mixture into a roll, and wrap it in parchment paper or waxed paper, twisting the ends to seal them. Store the Lavender Dill Butter in the refrigerator or freezer until needed. Makes approximately 1 cup.

Recipe Tested in the Kitchen of Julie Kampling

Garlic Mashed Potatoes with Fresh Chives & Lavender

Potatoes don't have to be boring anymore! I added garlic, chives, and lavender to my basic mashed potatoes recipe, and the result was phenomenal! Now, your family will applaud whenever they hear that mashed potatoes are being served.

3 pounds red-skinned potatoes

4 garlic cloves, minced

1/4 cup butter

1 tsp sea salt

1/2 cup low-fat milk

1/4 tsp fresh-ground black pepper

1/4 tsp Organic Culinary Lavender Buds

1 tsp fresh chives, chopped very fine

Wash and scrub the potatoes. Cut the potatoes into chunks, and place them in a large pot. Cover the potato chunks with cold water; the pot should be about 2/3 full. Bring the potatoes to a slow boil over medium-high heat, and cook, uncovered, until they are tender, but not mushy. Drain the water from the potatoes. Either transfer the potatoes to a large bowl or continue to work in the pot.

Variation

If you desire a creamier mashed potato dish, just use Half & Half instead of milk and add an additional 1 Tbsp of butter.

Add the garlic, butter, salt, milk, pepper, and lavender buds. Using an electric mixer or potato masher, whip or mash until all of the ingredients are thoroughly mixed and the potatoes are the consistency that you prefer. If the potatoes seem dry, add a few Tbsp of milk. Sprinkle with the chives, and serve. Makes approximately 8 servings.

Chef's Comments

If you don't need the full 8 servings, this recipe can be easily halved. Also, any leftovers can be refrigerated and reheated to enjoy the next day.

Years ago, my husband bought me an unusual gift, which has since become a treasure in our kitchen: a garlic press! This tool minces the garlic quickly and effortlessly, saving you from peeling and mincing the garlic by hand. This handy tool can be found at gourmet markets or online, and I highly recommend that every cook have one.

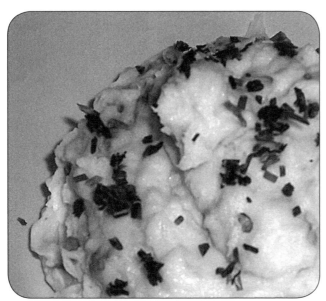

Photo Courtesy of Valerie Harms

Recipe Tested in the Kitchen of Valerie Harms

Rosemary & Lavender Roasted New Potatoes

These potatoes blend together two of my all-time favorite culinary herbs: rosemary and lavender. The taste is outstanding, and the aroma that wafts through the kitchen while they are baking is utterly fabulous.

3 pounds new potatoes OR small red-skinned potatoes

1 Tbsp extra-virgin olive oil, plus 3 Tbsp, separated

6 Tbsp butter

1/3 cup fresh-squeezed lemon juice

2 tsp fresh-grated lemon zest (see zesting tips on page 250)

1 tsp dried rosemary OR 2 tsp fresh rosemary

1 tsp Organic Culinary Lavender Buds

salt (to taste)

fresh-ground black pepper (to taste)

Preheat the oven to 375°F.

Wash and scrub the potatoes, and cut them into quarters. Drizzle 1 Tbsp of olive oil in the bottom of a 9-inch x 13-inch baking dish. Arrange the potatoes in the baking dish in a single layer.

In a small saucepan, combine together the remaining 3 Tbsp of olive oil, butter, lemon juice, and lemon zest, and heat, stirring frequently, just until the butter is melted.

Pour the butter mixture over the potatoes, and then sprinkle them with the rosemary, lavender buds, salt, and pepper. Bake at 375° for 35–45 minutes or until lightly brown. Makes approximately 6–8 servings.

Chef's Comments

These Rosemary & Lavender Roasted New Potatoes complement just about any recipe for chicken, fish, or steak; plus, they make a great addition to breakfast or brunch. Just cut the potatoes a little smaller when serving them with a morning meal.

∽✦∾

If you choose to use fresh rosemary in this recipe, it can be left whole or chopped. As with all culinary herbs, chopping them before adding them to your culinary recipes releases their essential oils, which provides more intense flavor.

∽✦∾

New potatoes are actually "early harvested" red-skinned potatoes. They are small, very moist, and tender. If you cannot find new potatoes, you can use regular red-skinned potatoes—just make sure you choose ones that are small in size.

Recipe Tested in the Kitchen of Doreen Weisgerber

Baked Sweet Potatoes with Lavender Cinnamon Sugar

Years ago, I lived in Abilene, Texas, and it was there that I tasted my first baked sweet potato. Ever since then, I have preferred the taste of a sweet potato over "common" potatoes. My Baked Sweet Potatoes with Lavender Cinnamon Sugar recipe is a delectable side dish for either chicken or beef, and the Lavender Cinnamon Sugar makes this the best way to eat a sweet potato.

4 large sweet potatoes
4 Tbsp butter

Lavender Cinnamon Sugar
3 Tbsp granulated sugar
2 Tbsp packed brown sugar
1 tsp Organic Culinary Lavender Buds
1 1/2 tsp cinnamon

Preheat the oven to 400°F.

Bake the sweet potatoes on a foil-lined cookie sheet for 45–75 minutes. (Larger sweet potatoes will take longer to cook.) The potato is done when the outside is crisp and the inside is soft. If you want to be sure the potato is fully baked, slice it open; it is ready when the center is soft and the natural sugars have caramelized and charred the inside of the skin.

While the sweet potatoes are baking, combine both sugars, along with the lavender buds and cinnamon, in a small bowl. Mix well.

Remove the potatoes from the oven, and slice them down the center. Top each sweet potato with 1 Tbsp of butter. Sprinkle them with the Lavender Cinnamon Sugar, and serve. Makes 4 servings.

Photo Courtesy of Lois Feldbush

Fascinating Facts

Even though the names "sweet potato" and "yam" are often used interchangeably in the United States, the two are botanically unrelated.

Since their flavors are similar, either one will work beautifully in this recipe and taste equally as good.

Recipe Tested in the Kitchen of Lois Feldbush

Lavender Lane

Soups & Stews

French Onion & Lavender Soup

Whether served as an appetizer or as a meal, French onion soup always seems to hit the spot. The addition of lavender, though, gives this timeless classic a very distinguished flavor and moves it into a category all its own.

6 Tbsp butter, cubed

5 large sweet yellow onions, thinly sliced

2 garlic cloves, minced

2 Tbsp all-purpose flour

1/2 cup dry white wine

3 cups beef stock

1 1/2 cups cold water

1 tsp Organic Culinary Lavender Buds

1/2 tsp salt

1/2 tsp fresh-ground black pepper

Garnish

3 Tbsp butter, softened

6 thick slices of crusty French bread

3 cups Swiss cheese, shredded

In a medium-size stockpot, heat the butter over low heat, and sauté the onions and garlic for about 20–30 minutes or until the onions are softened. Sprinkle the flour over the onions, and increase the heat to medium. Cook a few minutes longer, stirring constantly, until the flour turns brown in color.

Add the wine, and bring the mixture to boil for a few minutes, which allows the alcohol to evaporate. Add the beef stock, water, lavender buds, salt, and pepper. Bring the soup back to a boil, and then reduce the heat, cover, and simmer for 20 minutes.

Photo Courtesy of Lois Feldbush

In the meantime, to make the garnish, turn the oven to "broil." Spread the butter over the bread slices, and place them, buttered side up, on a cookie sheet. Toast the bread under the broiler—keeping it quite far away from the heat. (You may have to move your rack to the middle of the oven.) Watch the bread continuously to avoid burning—it takes just a few moments for it to toast. Remove the toasted bread from the oven, allow to cool, and break into pieces.

Preheat the oven to 400°F. When the soup is done cooking, spoon it into individual ovenproof bowls, and top with the toasted bread. Sprinkle the shredded Swiss cheese over the toast in each bowl. Place the bowls on a cookie sheet, and bake at 400° until the cheese is bubbly and golden brown, about 10–15 minutes. Serve immediately. Makes approximately 6 servings.

Recipe Tested in the Kitchen of Lois Feldbush

Parmesan & Lavender Roasted Tomato Soup

It's hard to imagine that a handful of vegetables could add up to so much flavor! This soup is fantastic served piping hot with fresh-grated Parmesan cheese and a few crispy croutons sprinkled on top, but it is equally delicious served cold. The secret is in the roasting, which helps bring out the natural flavors of the ingredients.

2 pounds Roma tomatoes

8 garlic cloves, minced

1 medium yellow onion, quartered

1 small red pepper, seeded and quartered

3 Tbsp extra-virgin olive oil

sea salt (to taste)

fresh-ground black pepper (to taste)

2 1/4 cups chicken stock

1/4 cup cream

1/4 cup fresh basil, chopped

1 Tbsp Organic Culinary Lavender Buds, chopped

1 tsp granulated sugar

1/2 Tbsp balsamic vinegar

2 Tbsp fresh-grated Parmesan cheese

garlic croutons (for garnish—optional)

additional fresh-grated Parmesan cheese (for garnish—optional)

Variation

To make a vegetarian version of this soup, simply use vegetable stock instead of the chicken stock.

Preheat the oven to 375°F. Score an "X" on the side of each tomato. In a large soup pot, boil some water, and place the tomatoes in it for about 30 seconds. Drain the tomatoes in a large colander, and immediately rinse them with cold water. The skins should be already peeling up from where the X was. Peel the skins away from the tomatoes. Discard the skins. Cut the tomatoes in quarters, and place them on a baking sheet.

Add the garlic, onion, and peppers to the tomatoes, and drizzle with the olive oil, turning the vegetables over, as needed, until everything is well coated. (Or the vegetables can be placed in a bowl to toss with the oil. Then spread them onto the sheet.) Sprinkle with salt and pepper. Roast the tomatoes and vegetables at 375° for about 45 minutes or until the tomatoes start to collapse and the onions begin to caramelize. Remove from the oven, and cool slightly.

Place the roasted tomatoes and vegetables into a food processor or blender, and pulse until smooth. Add the remaining ingredients, and blend again until smooth. Return the soup to a pot, and heat over medium heat until the soup begins to bubble. Season with additional salt and pepper, to taste. Garnish with garlic croutons and additional fresh-grated Parmesan cheese, if desired. Makes approximately 3–4 servings.

Photo Courtesy of Debbie Walter

Recipe Tested in the Kitchen of Debbie Walter

Lavender "Baked Potato" Soup with Bacon

My Lavender "Baked Potato" Soup with Bacon is just wonderful served piping hot on a chilly day. The "baked" part of this recipe's name comes from the fact that the soup's taste resembles a "loaded" baked potato, which is usually piled high with sour cream, cheese, and bacon. This soup is a snap to make, and the delicate lavender flavor offers an unexpected yet intriguing taste that is nothing short of extraordinary.

6 strips bacon

2 medium red-skinned potatoes

2 cups water

2 Tbsp butter

1 small yellow onion, finely chopped

2 Tbsp all-purpose flour

1/2 tsp Organic Culinary Lavender Buds, ground

1/4–1/2 tsp garlic salt (to taste)

1/4–1/2 tsp fresh-ground black pepper (to taste)

2 1/2 cups low-fat milk

1/2 tsp granulated sugar

1/3 cup reduced-fat sour cream

3/4 cup sharp cheddar cheese, shredded

In a large frying pan, cook the bacon until crisp. Place the cooked bacon on a cookie sheet lined with paper towels to absorb any fat. Set aside.

Scrub the potatoes, and cut them into 1-inch cubes. In a large soup pot, bring the water to a boil, and cook the potatoes until tender. Remove from the heat, and set aside—do not drain.

In a small frying pan, heat the butter over medium heat, and sauté the onion, stirring frequently, until the onion is translucent and tender, but not brown. Add the flour to the pan, along with the ground lavender buds, garlic salt, and pepper. Mix well, and continue to cook for an additional 2 minutes, stirring constantly.

Return the potatoes to the stove, and heat over medium-high heat. Add the onion mixture, milk, and sugar. Stir well, and allow the soup to come to a boil. Add the sour cream and cheese. Crumble the bacon, and add it to the soup. Mix well. Reduce the heat to low, and simmer for 15–20 minutes, stirring frequently. Makes approximately 4 servings.

Photo Courtesy of Lois Feldbush

Recipe Tested in the Kitchen of Lois Feldbush

Italian Wedding Soup with Lavender Mini-Meatballs

Anyone who lives in the Midwest is probably quite familiar with this soup, which is a staple in many restaurants. My version includes delicious mini-meatballs that are bursting with flavor from herbs and cheeses. My family and I enjoy this soup at lunchtime, but it also makes an excellent light dinner, especially when paired with Lavender Olive Bread, which can be found on page 204.

1/2 pound ground turkey

1/3 cup bread crumbs

1 egg, slightly beaten

1 Tbsp onion, finely minced

1 tsp Herbs de Provence (with lavender)

2 tsp chicken-flavored soup base, plus
    2 Tbsp, separated

1 Tbsp asiago cheese, finely grated

1 Tbsp fresh-grated Parmesan cheese,
    finely grated

1 Tbsp olive oil

6 cups water

1/4 tsp garlic powder

1/4 tsp fresh-ground black pepper

1/2 cup uncooked acini di pepe pasta

2 cups baby spinach leaves, thinly sliced

additional fresh-grated Parmesan cheese (for garnish—optional)

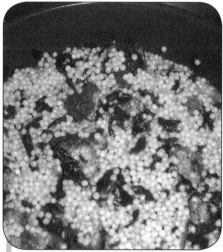

Photo Courtesy of Tony Kampling

In a small bowl, combine together the turkey, bread crumbs, egg, onion, Herbs de Provence, 2 tsp of the soup base, and both cheeses. Mix all ingredients until well incorporated, and then shape into 1/2-inch meatballs. In a nonstick frying pan, heat 1 Tbsp olive oil over medium heat, and lightly brown the meatballs, turning them frequently, for 3–4 minutes. Remove the pan from the heat, and drain any oil from the meatballs.

In a large soup pot, combine together the water with the remaining 2 Tbsp of the soup base, along with the garlic powder and pepper. Bring the mixture to a boil. Reduce the heat to medium-high, add the meatballs and the pasta. Cook the soup, uncovered, for 10 minutes or until the pasta is tender.

Reduce the heat to low, add the spinach leaves, and simmer for 5 minutes or until the spinach is tender. Garnish with fresh-grated Parmesan cheese, if desired. Makes approximately 6–8 servings.

Chef's Comments

Herbs de Provence can be purchased at most specialty stores or online at www.AllThingsLavender.com.

You can also create your own Herbs de Provence by following the recipe on page 19.

Chicken soup base is a handy substitution for chicken bouillon cubes. The soup base, which includes chicken fat and a savory seasoning blend, provides a flavorful foundation for soups and broths. It can usually be found next to the bouillon cubes at most supermarkets.

Recipe Tested in the Kitchen of Tony Kampling

Lavender Minestrone Soup

A classic Italian favorite, minestrone is commonly made with fresh seasonal vegetables. If you are able to use farm-fresh ingredients, the taste is even better. Feel free to experiment by adding vegetables or substituting others for the ones used here. Perfect for a cold or rainy day, this hearty soup will be enjoyed down to the last spoonful.

1 1/2 tsp extra-virgin olive oil

1 small white onion, minced

1/4 cup celery, minced

2 garlic cloves, minced

2 1/2 cups vegetable broth

2 1/2 cups water

1/2 cup fresh parsley, chopped OR 2 Tbsp dried parsley

1 tsp Organic Culinary Lavender Buds

1/2 tsp dried basil OR 1 1/2 tsp fresh basil

3/4 tsp dried oregano OR 1 1/2 tsp fresh oregano

1 can (15 oz. size) red kidney beans, drained

1 can (15.5 oz. size) cannellini beans OR great northern beans, drained

1 can (14.5 oz. size) diced fire-roasted tomatoes (we prefer Hunt's brand)

1/2 cup zucchini, chopped

1/2 cup frozen cut Italian green beans

1 small potato, diced

1/4 cup carrots, diced

2 cups baby spinach leaves, chopped

1/2 cup uncooked ditalini pasta (see the photo on the next page)

1 tsp sea salt

1/2 tsp fresh-ground black pepper
fresh-grated Parmesan cheese (for garnish)

In a soup pot, heat the oil over medium heat, and sauté the onion, celery, and garlic for about 5–7 minutes. Add the vegetable broth, water, and spices, except the salt and pepper. Stir in the beans and vegetables, except the spinach. Bring the soup to a boil, reduce the heat to low, cover, and simmer for 18 minutes.

Photo Courtesy of Lois Feldbush

Add the spinach and pasta, and stir. Re-cover, and cook for an additional 20–25 minutes or until the pasta is tender. Season the soup with the salt and pepper, and top with fresh-grated Parmesan cheese. Makes approximately 4–6 servings.

Ditalini Pasta

Recipe Tested in the Kitchen of Lois Feldbush

Herbed Cheese Tortellini Soup

This comforting soup can be made in a jiffy. Even though this is a reduced-fat version of the classic, it is still quite flavorful and satisfying.

8 cups low-salt chicken broth

1/2 cup carrots, thinly sliced

1 small yellow onion, finely chopped

1/2 cup celery, thinly sliced

2 cups dried, uncooked cheese-filled
    tortellini

1/2 tsp dried thyme

1/4 tsp fresh-ground black pepper

1/2 tsp Organic Culinary Lavender Buds

2 Tbsp fresh Italian parsley, chopped (for
    garnish)

Variation

This soup can easily be made into a vegetarian version. Simply use vegetable broth instead of the chicken broth, and add 1 Tbsp of butter.

Top with fresh-grated Parmesan cheese for a real Italian treat.

Pour the broth into a medium-size soup pot, and bring to a boil over high heat. Reduce the heat to medium. Add all of the remaining ingredients except for the parsley. Bring the soup back to boiling over medium heat. Reduce the heat to low, cover, and simmer for 20 minutes or until the pasta is tender. Serve in soup bowls, and garnish with the fresh parsley. Makes approximately 6–8 servings.

Chef's Comments

To make this soup more stew-like, simply double the amounts for the vegetables.

Since this soup just hints at lavender, it can be paired with a lavender-flavored side without becoming too overpowering.

For a light meal, try the soup with a small garden salad and the Herbal Butter Garlic Bread found on page 199 or the Lavender Focaccia Bread on page 202.

Photo Courtesy of Debbie Walter

Recipe Tested in the Kitchen of Debbie Walter

Lavender, Broccoli & Cheddar Soup

Whether you need a mouthwatering appetizer or a hearty supper, soup fits the bill—and this recipe is no exception. The lavender flavor transforms this traditional soup into an ideal first course, and yet, when the same recipe is paired with multigrain bread, it becomes a flavorful and filling meal.

1 pkg (10 oz. size) frozen chopped broccoli, thawed

2 Tbsp butter

2 Tbsp extra-virgin olive oil

1 garlic clove, minced

1/2 small sweet yellow onion, minced (it should measure about 1/3 cup)

1 cup Half & Half

1 Tbsp Organic Culinary Lavender Buds

1 cup water

1/4 cup carrots, grated

1 cup (8 oz.) Velveeta cheese, cubed

1/4 tsp sea salt

1/4 tsp fresh-ground black pepper

1 cup extra-sharp cheddar cheese, shredded

In a small frying pan, heat the butter and olive oil over low heat, and sauté the garlic and onion for about 8 minutes. Add the thawed broccoli to the onions and garlic. Mix well, and set aside.

In a medium-size soup pot, combine the Half & Half and lavender buds. Bring the mixture to a boil over medium heat. Once the Half & Half begins to boil, immediately reduce the heat to low. Simmer for 5 minutes, stirring frequently. Remove from the heat, and strain the lavender buds from the Half & Half. Discard the lavender buds, and return the lavender-infused Half & Half to the soup pot.

Photo Courtesy of Laura Cesaro

Add the water, carrots, Velveeta, salt, and pepper. Mix well. Stir in the broccoli mixture. Return the soup to a boil, and then reduce the heat to low, stirring frequently. Once the Velveeta is completely melted, add the shredded cheddar cheese. Stir well, and continue to simmer over low heat until the soup thickens, about 5 minutes. Serve with your favorite bread or crackers. Makes approximately 4–6 servings.

Recipe Tested in the Kitchen of Laura Cesaro

Lemon & Lavender Lentil Soup

This is a unique version of a traditional Lebanese soup. You will be pleasantly surprised by the way the flavors mingle together to create such delicious flavor. It tastes superb served with pita bread, or try it with my Lavender Feta Fattoush with Toasted Pita, see the recipe on page 158, to make a complete meal.

1/2 bunch fresh cilantro, stems removed

4 garlic cloves, minced

1 1/4 tsp Organic Culinary Lavender Buds

2 Tbsp extra-virgin olive oil, plus 2 Tbsp, separated

1/8 tsp salt

1 large yellow onion, finely chopped

1/2 pound lentils, washed and drained

1/2 tsp cinnamon

4 cups vegetable stock

2 cups water

1 can (14.5 oz. size) diced fire-roasted tomatoes (we prefer Hunt's brand)

1/2 cup carrots, sliced 1-inch-thick (about 1 large)

1 medium potato, cubed

1/4 cup fresh-squeezed lemon juice

1 pkg (4 oz. size) baby spinach leaves, thinly sliced

additional salt (to taste—optional)

fresh-ground black pepper (to taste)

lemon wedges (for garnish)

Place the cilantro, garlic, lavender buds, 2 Tbsp of the olive oil, and the 1/8 tsp salt in a food processor or blender. Pulse until the ingredients form a paste, scraping down the sides of the container with a spatula as needed. Set aside.

In a large soup pot, heat the remaining 2 Tbsp of olive oil over medium heat, and sauté the onion until it becomes a light brown. Add the lentils, cinnamon, vegetable stock, water, and tomatoes, and stir well. Cook, uncovered, over medium heat for 45 minutes, stirring occasionally.

Photo Courtesy of Heidi Bitsoli

Reduce the heat to low. Add the cilantro mixture, carrots, and potato. Cook, uncovered, for about 25 more minutes or until the lentils are creamy. Add the lemon juice and spinach, and cook for an additional 10 minutes. Season with additional salt, if desired, and pepper, to taste. Garnish with lemon wedges. Makes approximately 6–8 servings.

Recipe Tested in the Bitsoli Kitchen

Stuffed Red Pepper Soup with Lavender

This soup version of my mother's famous stuffed peppers uses ground turkey instead of beef. Plus, I've added the taste of lavender, through the Herbs de Provence, which makes this already wonderful soup absolutely fabulous.

1 pound ground turkey

6 cups water

1 chicken bouillon cube

1/2 cup yellow onion, diced

1 can (14.5 oz. size) diced fire-roasted tomatoes (we prefer Hunt's brand)

1 can (14.5 oz. size) tomato sauce (we prefer Hunt's brand)

2/3 cup uncooked brown rice

1 large red bell pepper, chopped (about 1 cup)

1 garlic clove, minced

2 Tbsp packed brown sugar

1 tsp salt

1/2 tsp fresh-ground black pepper

1 tsp Herbs de Provence (with lavender)

In a large soup pot, brown the ground turkey over medium heat. Drain the fat from the turkey with a strainer, and return the meat to the pot. Add the water and bouillon, and stir over medium heat for a few minutes until the bouillon is completely dissolved.

Add the remaining ingredients, and stir until well incorporated. Bring the soup to a boil, stir, and reduce the heat to low. Cover, and simmer for 35 minutes or until the rice is tender. Makes approximately 6–8 servings.

Chef's Comments

Herbs de Provence can be purchased at most specialty stores or online at www.AllThingsLavender.com.

You can also create your own Herbs de Provence by following the recipe on page 19.

Photo Courtesy of Julie Kampling

Recipe Tested in the Kitchen of Julie Kampling

Lavender Lamb Stew

This is one of those dishes that came about purely by accident. Motivated by his appetite, my husband created a stew by "throwing" together whatever ingredients we had in the house. The result was phenomenal. My entire family is still intrigued by this stew's rich flavor and wholesome goodness— it has become one of our favorite meals.

2 pounds lamb stew meat

1 Tbsp olive oil

1 cup water

1/4 tsp garlic salt

1/2 tsp fresh-ground black pepper

1 tsp Organic Culinary Lavender Buds

1 Tbsp Worcestershire sauce

2 small yellow onions, diced

2 stalks celery, diced

1 1/4 cups baby carrots, diced

2 medium potatoes, diced

1 can (15 oz. size) black beans, with juice

Cut the lamb meat into 2-inch or 3-inch cubes. In a large stockpot, heat the oil over medium-high heat, and brown the meat.

When the lamb is browned, add the water, garlic salt, pepper, lavender buds, and Worcestershire sauce. Mix well. Add the diced vegetables and black beans, and stir together until well blended.

Continue to heat the stew over medium-high heat, just until it begins to bubble. Cover the stockpot, and turn the heat to low. Simmer the stew, stirring occasionally, for about 20 minutes or until the potatoes and carrots are "al dente." Makes approximately 4–6 servings.

Chef's Comments

Complete this tasty meal with the Herbal Butter Garlic Bread found on page 199 or the Lavender Focaccia Bread on page 202.

Black beans add not only wonderful flavor but also extra protein to this stew; plus, they are high in fiber, low in fat, and a great source of iron.

Recipe Tested in the Kitchen of David Stockton

Hearty Lavender Beef Stew

My Hearty Lavender Beef Stew is great for busy days when there isn't much time to cook. It can be prepared in less than 15 minutes, and since it cooks in the Crock-Pot, it's basically carefree—yet it tastes as if you tended to it for hours. Best of all, the pleasant aroma greets you with a warm welcome, especially after a long day.

1 pound beef (rump roast OR chuck roast), cut into 2-inch chunks

2 Tbsp all-purpose flour

2 tsp Herbs de Provence (with lavender)

1/4 tsp salt

1/4 tsp fresh-ground black pepper

1 tsp Worcestershire sauce

1 can (14.5 oz. size) diced fire-roasted tomatoes (we prefer Hunt's brand)

1 small yellow onion, diced

1 large carrot, peeled and sliced 1-inch-thick

1 large potato, peeled and diced into 1-inch cubes

1/2 cup frozen green beans

1/2 cup frozen sweet corn

1 cup water

Place the meat in a Crock-Pot. Sprinkle it with the flour, herbs, salt, and pepper. Stir until the meat is well coated.

Add the remaining ingredients, and mix until well blended. Cover, and cook the stew on low heat for 8–10 hours or on high heat for 4–6 hours.

When the stew is finished cooking, break up the chunks of meat with a fork. Stir well just before serving. Serve with your favorite bread or biscuits or with Grandma's Cheddar & Herb Buttermilk Biscuits, which can be found on page 200. Makes approximately 4–5 servings.

Chef's Comments

Herbs de Provence can be purchased at most specialty stores or online at www.AllThingsLavender.com.

You can also create your own Herbs de Provence by following the recipe on page 19.

Photo Courtesy of Valerie Harms

Recipe Tested in the Kitchen of Valerie Harms

Lavender Turkey & Dumpling Stew

Nothing quite warms your spirit like this hearty stew on a cold day. I like to use turkey—a wonderful comfort food—instead of chicken, but either one can be used with equally good results. The delectable flavor combination of the lavender and chives transforms this simple stew into something truly scrumptious.

Stew

16–20 oz. boneless, skinless turkey breast

1 quart (4 cups) low-sodium chicken broth

2 cups water

1/2 tsp Organic Culinary Lavender Buds

1/8 tsp fresh-ground black pepper

1/8 tsp garlic powder

1 large yellow onion, cut into small chunks

2 stalks celery, sliced 1/4-inch-thick

2 large carrots, sliced 1/2-inch-thick

Dumplings

1 2/3 cup baking mix (we prefer Bisquick Heart Smart Baking Mix)

1/2 cup skim milk

1/4 cup fresh chives, thinly sliced

Cut the turkey breast cutlets into 2-inch pieces. Combine together the turkey and all the other ingredients for the stew in a large soup pot. Cook over medium-high heat, stirring frequently, until the soup begins to boil. Reduce the heat to low, cover, and simmer for 20 minutes or until the turkey is fully cooked and the carrots are tender.

Mix together the ingredients for the dumplings until completely moistened and a soft dough forms. Increase the heat of the stew to boiling. Drop the dumpling dough, by small spoonfuls, onto the top of the boiling stew. Cook, uncovered, for an additional 10 minutes. Remove from the heat, and serve. Makes approximately 6–8 servings.

Chef's Comments

If you prefer a thicker broth for this stew, simply combine 1 part cornstarch with 2 parts cold water, and stir until smooth. Slowly pour the mixture into the soup, a little at a time, while stirring constantly and checking the consistency. Stop adding the cornstarch mixture when the desired thickness is achieved.

Photo Courtesy of Debbie Walter

Recipe Tested in the Kitchen of Debbie Walter

Lavender Lane

Salsa, Salads & Dressings

Lavender Cilantro Garden Salsa

There is nothing quite like homemade salsa. My friend Dee taught me how to make salsa almost 10 years ago, and we make it often, using a variety of different ingredients every time. This is a wonderful recipe that blends together some of our favorite tastes, along with a hint of lavender. The best thing about homemade salsa is that it can be made year-round, yet it tastes as if you had picked everything fresh from the garden.

1 large Vidalia onion OR other sweet onion

1 bell pepper (yellow or green, your preference)

4–8 jalapeño pepper slices (we use Vlasic's zesty jalapeño pepper slices)

1 bunch fresh cilantro leaves

1 can (28–32 oz. size) whole tomatoes

1/4 cup fresh-squeezed lemon juice

2 garlic cloves, finely minced

1/2 Tbsp sea salt

1/2 tsp Organic Culinary Lavender Buds

Chop the first 4 ingredients together in a food processor. Add the tomatoes, lemon juice, garlic, salt, and lavender buds, and chop some more until the salsa is the consistency that you prefer. Refrigerate for 1 hour before serving. Makes approximately 2 cups.

Chef's Comments

The more jalapeño peppers you add, the hotter the salsa will be. For a mild salsa, add very little.

This salsa can also be hand-chopped, if you prefer.

Photo Courtesy of Arlene Hicks

Recipe Tested in the Kitchen of Arlene Hicks

Mango Lavender Salsa

This fresh, sweet salsa adds a unique contrast to spicy grilled fish, chicken, or steak, and it's equally delicious when served with tortilla chips.

2 ripe mangoes, peeled and finely diced (about 2 cups)

1/2 cup fresh pineapple, peeled, cored, and finely diced

1 small cucumber, finely chopped

1 medium-size red bell pepper, finely chopped

1/2 medium red onion, finely chopped

3–6 jalapeño pepper slices, finely chopped (we use Vlasic's zesty jalapeño pepper slices)

4 Tbsp fresh cilantro leaves, finely chopped

4 Tbsp fresh-squeezed lime juice

1/4 tsp salt

1/2 tsp Organic Culinary Lavender Buds

1/2 tsp dried mint leaves

Combine all of the ingredients in a bowl, and mix well. Refrigerate for 1 hour and stir well before serving. Makes approximately 3 cups.

Chef's Comments

The more jalapeño peppers you add, the hotter the salsa will be. For a mild salsa, add very little.

If the salsa turns out to be too hot for your liking, it can be tempered by adding some diced avocado.

Photo Courtesy of Maribeth Criscenti

Recipe Tested in the Kitchen of Maribeth Criscenti

Lavender Gazpacho Salsa

Originally from Spain, Gazpacho is a cold, raw vegetable soup that can be prepared many different ways. This delicious concoction assumed a completely new identity when I turned it into a mouthwatering salsa. It is wonderful when made with fresh seasonal vegetables and scooped up with blue corn tortilla chips. Or, for a change of pace, try serving it alongside your favorite grilled chicken or seafood. Simply fantastico!

5 medium tomatoes, peeled, seeded, and diced

1 medium cucumber, peeled, seeded, and diced

1/2 medium red onion, diced

1/2 green bell pepper, diced

2 cups frozen sweet corn kernels

1 poblano chili pepper, finely diced (if preferred, you can use 1 jalapeño pepper instead)

1/2 cup fresh cilantro leaves, finely chopped

Lavender Gazpacho Salsa Marinade (see the recipe on the next page)

Combine together the tomatoes, cucumber, onion, bell pepper, corn, chili pepper, and cilantro in a large bowl. Prepare the Lavender Gazpacho Salsa Marinade, and pour it over the vegetables. Mix well. Cover, and refrigerate for at least 4 hours or overnight. Makes approximately 8 servings.

Lavender Gazpacho Salsa Marinade

1/4 cup fresh-squeezed lime juice

1 Tbsp extra-virgin olive oil

1 garlic clove, minced

1/4 tsp sea salt

1/4 tsp fresh-ground black pepper

1/4 tsp chili powder

1/4 tsp Organic Culinary Lavender
   Buds, chopped

In a small mixing bowl, combine together all the ingredients. Whisk until well blended.

Chef's Comments

If the salsa is too hot for your taste, diced avocados can be added to help temper the heat.

The easiest way to peel tomatoes is to blanch them in boiling water for 30 seconds, and then immediately transfer them to a bowl of cold water for 30 seconds.

Photo Courtesy of Maribeth Criscenti

Recipe Tested in the Kitchen of Maribeth Criscenti

Lavender Cranberry Chutney

While canned cranberry sauces are quick and easy, they can't compare to the flavor and pizzazz of my Lavender Cranberry Chutney. Perfect for Thanksgiving—especially if turkey is the main course—this savory chutney also tastes great on sandwiches, toast, and crackers.

2 cups cranberries, fresh OR frozen

1/2 cup granulated sugar

1/4 cup packed brown sugar

1/4 cup golden raisins

1 tsp ground cinnamon

1/2 tsp Organic Culinary Lavender Buds

1/2 tsp ground cloves

1/2 cup water

1/2 cup apples, peeled, cored, and chopped (Gala, Golden Delicious, or
    Jonathan apples work the best)

1/2 cup yellow onion, chopped

1/4 cup celery, chopped

Combine all of the ingredients in a large saucepan, except for the onion and celery, and bring to boil. Stir well. Reduce the heat to low, and simmer, stirring frequently, for about 10–15 minutes.

Add the onion and celery, and continue to simmer, stirring occasionally, for an additional 10 minutes or until the sauce thickens. Chill 4–6 hours before serving. Store in the refrigerator in an airtight container for up to 1 week. Makes approximately 6–8 servings.

Variation

For a real treat, try this Baked Brie Cheese with Lavender Cranberry Chutney...

Preheat the oven to 350°F. Place an 8 oz. round Brie cheese in the center of a well-oiled baking dish. Bake, uncovered, at 350° for 8–10 minutes or until the cheese is partially melted. Spoon about 1 cup of warm Lavender Cranberry Chutney over the cheese. Then sprinkle with 1/4 cup of walnuts, pecans, or almonds, if desired. Serve with a toasted baguette or crackers.

Photo Courtesy of Debbie Walter

Recipe Tested in the Kitchen of Debbie Walter

Chicken Apple Salad with Lavender Candied Pecans

The sweet, crispy texture of the Granny Smith apples together with the mild, smoky flavor of the blue cheese taste incredibly decadent in this salad. The Lavender Candied Pecans offer a crunchy surprise and are even delicious enough to serve on their own.

2 boneless, skinless chicken breasts, cut in half

1/3 cup fresh-squeezed lemon juice

sea salt & fresh-ground black pepper (to taste)

12 cups mixed salad greens

2 Granny Smith apples, peeled, cored, and thinly sliced

1/2 red onion, thinly sliced

3/4 cup crumbled blue cheese

1 cup Lavender Candied Pecans (see the recipe on the next page)

balsamic dressing (your favorite brand)

Photo Courtesy of Julie Kampling

Lightly coat a frying pan with olive oil or vegetable cooking spray. Heat the pan for 1–2 minutes over medium heat. Lay the chicken breasts in the pan. Pour the lemon juice over the chicken, and then sprinkle with the salt and pepper, to taste. Reduce the heat to low, cover the pan, and cook the chicken for 6–8 minutes per side or until thoroughly cooked. Transfer the chicken to a cutting board, allow to cool slightly, and cut into slices.

Toss together the salad greens, apple slices, onion, and blue cheese. Arrange the salad on individual dinner plates. Divide the chicken evenly over the salad greens. Sprinkle with the Lavender Candied Pecans, and serve with your favorite balsamic dressing. Makes approximately 4–6 servings.

Lavender Candied Pecans

1 cup granulated sugar

1 tsp salt

2 tsp Organic Culinary Lavender
    Buds

1 tsp ground cinnamon

1 egg white, room temperature

1 Tbsp water

1 pound whole pecan halves

Preheat the oven to 300°F. In a spice grinder, pulse together the sugar, salt, and lavender buds until well ground. In a bowl, combine the sugar mixture with the cinnamon; set aside. In another bowl, beat together the egg white and water until frothy, but not stiff. Add the pecans, and mix until well blended. Sprinkle the sugar and cinnamon mixture over the

Photo Courtesy of Julie Kampling

pecans, and stir until well coated. Evenly spread the pecans onto a foil-lined baking sheet. Bake for 30 minutes at 300°. Turn the pecans every 10 minutes while they are baking. Remove the pecans from the oven, and separate them as they cool. Store the pecans in a tightly closed container. Makes approximately 1 pound.

Recipe Tested in the Kitchen of Julie Kampling

Mandarin Salad with Lavender Sesame Dressing

When I was a kid, my older sisters often treated me to a day of shopping at Hudson's, an upscale department store located in the Detroit area. Afterward, we would have lunch in the store's dining room, which served many family-favorite recipes—made with a gourmet spin. This salad is my sisters' adapted version of the one that Hudson's made famous, and the subtle hint of lavender gives the dressing incredible taste and appeal.

2 boneless, skinless chicken breasts
juice from 1/2 lemon
salt (to taste)
fresh-ground black pepper (to taste)
6 strips bacon
4 cups romaine lettuce, chopped
4 cups baby spinach leaves
1 can (11 oz. size) mandarin oranges, drained
1 can (8 oz. size) sliced water chestnuts, cut in half
1 1/2 cups frozen pea pods, thawed
Lavender Sesame Dressing (see the recipe on the next page)
1 1/2 cups chow mein noodles

Cut the chicken breasts in half, lengthwise. Lightly coat a frying pan with vegetable cooking spray. Heat the pan for 1–2 minutes over medium heat. Lay the chicken breasts in the pan. Pour the lemon juice over the chicken, and then sprinkle with the salt and pepper, to taste. Reduce the heat to low, cover the pan, and cook the chicken for 6–8 minutes per side or until thoroughly cooked. Transfer the chicken to a cutting board, and set aside.

In a large frying pan, cook the bacon until crisp. Place the cooked bacon on a cookie sheet lined with paper towels to absorb any fat. When the bacon cools, crumble it into pieces, and set aside. Mix together the lettuce, spinach, mandarin oranges, water chestnuts, pea pods, and bacon in a large salad bowl. Toss the salad with Lavender Sesame Dressing, to taste. Arrange the salad on individual dinner plates. Slice the chicken, and divide it evenly over the salad. Sprinkle with chow mein noodles, and serve! Makes approximately 4–6 servings.

Chef's Comments

To make onion juice, coarsely chop an onion, and then put it in your blender or food processor bowl. Blend or pulse until pureed, scraping down the sides of the bowl as needed. Pour the puree into a fine-mesh strainer, straining the liquid into a cup or bowl. Press down with a spatula to squeeze out the juice, and use immediately. It takes about 1 medium onion to make 3 Tbsp of onion juice.

To toast sesame seeds, place them in a nonstick skillet, and heat over medium heat, tossing often. Remove the seeds when they darken and become fragrant. Allow the seeds to cool before using. Store any unused seeds in a covered jar at room temperature.

Lavender Sesame Dressing

1/2 cup light honey
1/2 cup granulated sugar
2 tsp dry mustard
1 1/2 tsp salt
2/3 cup apple cider vinegar
3 Tbsp onion juice
2 tsp soy sauce
1 1/2 cups sesame oil
3 Tbsp toasted sesame seeds
1/2 tsp Organic Culinary Lavender
    Buds, ground

In a food processor or blender, pulse together the honey, sugar, mustard, salt, vinegar, onion juice, and soy sauce. Slowly add the sesame oil, a little at a time, mixing constantly until thick. Add the sesame seeds and ground lavender buds, and pulse until well blended. Unused dressing may be stored in the refrigerator for up to 1 week. Before using the dressing, allow it to reach room temperature and stir well. Makes approximately 3 cups.

Recipe Tested in the Kitchen of Judy Addabbo

Lavender Feta Fattoush with Toasted Pita

Imagine a salad made with crisp romaine, tomatoes, cucumbers, fresh mint, and feta cheese seasoned with a hint of culinary lavender. Now, add the crunch of toasted pita chips and a traditional Lebanese-style dressing. The result is a tangy and refreshing salad called fattoush. My entire family enjoys this light, healthy salad on a regular basis—and I'm sure yours will too.

2 hearts of romaine, chopped (about 6 cups)

1 cup cherry tomatoes, halved

1 cucumber, peeled and diced

1/2 small red onion, thinly sliced (about 1/3 cup)

1/4 cup fresh mint, finely chopped (about 1/2 a bunch)

1/4 cup fresh parsley, finely chopped (about 1/2 a bunch)

1 cup feta cheese

1/2 tsp Organic Culinary Lavender Buds

Fattoush Dressing (see the recipe on the next page)

1 1/2 cups toasted pita chips, crumbled (we prefer Stacy's brand)

Place the romaine, tomatoes, cucumber, onion, mint, and parsley in a large salad bowl. In a separate bowl, crumble together the feta cheese and lavender buds, and set aside.

Make the Fattoush Dressing. Add the feta cheese and crumbled pita chips to the salad, and then pour on the dressing. Toss until the romaine is well coated with the dressing. Serve immediately. Makes approximately 4–6 servings.

Fattoush Dressing

2 garlic cloves, finely
    minced
1/3 cup fresh-squeezed
    lemon juice
2 Tbsp rice wine vinegar
    OR red wine vinegar
2 Tbsp ground sumac
1/8 tsp fresh-ground
    black pepper
1/3 cup extra-virgin
    olive oil

To make the dressing, place all of the ingredients, except the olive oil, in a large bowl. Whisk together. Add the oil, a little at a time, and continue to whisk until the dressing is smooth.

Chef's Comments

If you'd rather toast your own pita bread, it's easy to do. Preheat the oven to 375°F. Take 2 pita rounds, and cut each into 6 triangles. Split each triangle in half to make 2 separate pieces. Place the pita bread in a single layer on a baking sheet, and bake until toasted, about 10 minutes. Remove the bread from the oven, turn over the pieces, and bake until the other side gets toasty. Cool the pita bread, and crumble over the salad.

What is sumac? The word sumac usually conjures up thoughts of poison sumac—especially to those in eastern North America, where the plant flourishes. But the sumac in this recipe has nothing to do with that surly little tree. Sumac spice comes from the nonpoisonous Sicilian sumac tree, which thrives in the Mediterranean region. The berries from the Sicilian sumac are dried and then ground, creating a reddish-colored spice that has a tangy, lemony flavor. We purchase our sumac at a Middle Eastern market, but it can also be found at most ethnic markets or online at www.zamourispices.com.

Recipe Tested in the Kitchen of Jan Wiley

Tabbouleh with Garlic & Lavender

Tabbouleh is a superb dish of Lebanese origin, and it contains wheat, parsley, tomatoes, and a host of other healthful ingredients. My version of this salad adds lavender, which flawlessly complements the medley of flavors that is tabbouleh. My family and I enjoy this tasty dish with toasted pita chips and fresh hummus, but it is delicious and filling enough to serve on its own.

1 cup bulgur wheat

1 cup hot water (hot from the tap works fine)

1 1/4 cups fresh parsley, finely chopped

1/4 cup fresh mint, chopped

1/3 cup green onion, finely chopped

3 garlic cloves, finely minced

1/2 tsp dried oregano

1/2 tsp Organic Culinary Lavender Buds, crushed OR chopped

1/4 tsp sea salt

1/8 tsp fresh-ground black pepper

1/2 cup fresh-squeezed lemon juice

1/4 cup extra-virgin olive oil

3 tomatoes, seeded and finely chopped

Soak the bulgur wheat in the hot water for 15–20 minutes. Drain any excess water from the bulgur wheat, and place the bulgur in a large mixing bowl.

Add the parsley, mint, onion, garlic, oregano, lavender buds, salt, and pepper, and mix well. Add the lemon juice, olive oil, and tomatoes, and blend well again. Refrigerate for 4 hours before serving. Mix before serving. Makes approximately 6 servings.

Photo Courtesy of Kim Parr

Recipe Tested in the Kitchen of Kim Parr

Citrus Herb Salad with Lavender Ginger Vinaigrette

Picture a salad that combines colorful citrus fruits, fresh green herbs, and toasted hazelnuts. Well, this cheerful Citrus Herb Salad has all those wonderful ingredients, plus the added zip of my Lavender Ginger Vinaigrette. Ideal for a summer's afternoon, this healthful salad is sure to become a favorite—especially for anyone who loves the zing of citrus.

1 pkg (4 oz. size) fresh herb salad mix (we prefer Earthbound Farm brand)

1/2 red onion, thinly sliced

1 blood orange, peeled OR 2 nectarines, cut off the core

1 small grapefruit, peeled

Lavender Ginger Vinaigrette (see the recipe on the next page)

1/3 cup crumbled blue cheese OR goat cheese

1/2 cup toasted hazelnuts

Place the salad greens and onion in a large salad bowl. Pull the orange and grapefruit apart into their natural segments. Using a sharp knife, cut away any tough membranes on the fruit segments, and then cut the segments in half. (If you are using nectarines instead of the orange, just cut the fruit flesh into large chunks.) Add the fruit to the salad greens.

Add the Lavender Ginger Vinaigrette dressing, to taste, and toss the salad. Divide the Citrus Herb Salad evenly on 4 plates, and top with crumbled blue cheese and toasted hazelnuts. Serve immediately. Makes 4 servings.

Lavender Ginger Vinaigrette

1/2 tsp Organic Culinary Lavender
   Buds

2 Tbsp Dijon mustard (preferably
   Grey Poupon brand)

1/2 cup honey

1/4 cup fresh-squeezed lime juice

2 Tbsp granulated sugar

1 Tbsp apple cider vinegar

2 Tbsp fresh-grated gingerroot

2 Tbsp sesame oil

salt and fresh-ground black pepper
   (to taste—optional)

In a spice grinder or a coffee grinder, chop the lavender buds until finely ground, and set aside. In a medium-size bowl or food processor, blend together all of the ingredients, including the ground lavender buds, until smooth. Season, to taste, with salt and pepper, if desired. Refrigerate for up to 1 week.

Photo Courtesy of Debbie Walter

Recipe Tested in the Kitchen of Debbie Walter

Spinach Salad with Toasted Pine Nuts & Lavender Raspberry Vinaigrette

This salad is rich in flavor and offers a sweet and savory surprise with each bite. If vine-ripened strawberries are in season, opt to use those first.

2/3 cup uncooked orzo pasta

1 cup pine nuts

Lavender Raspberry Vinaigrette (see the recipe on the next page)

1 pkg (10 oz. size) washed and ready-to-use baby spinach leaves

1 1/2 cups fresh strawberries, stemmed, washed, and sliced

1/2 small red onion, cut in thin slices

1/4 cup real bacon bits

1/3 cup feta cheese (optional)

Cook the orzo pasta according to the package's directions, and set aside.

To toast the pine nuts, place them in a dry nonstick pan, and heat them over medium heat, shaking every 30 seconds to evenly toast them. When the pine nuts are lightly browned, remove them from the heat. Allow nuts to cool before placing them in the salad.

Prepare the Lavender Raspberry Vinaigrette dressing, and set aside. Combine the spinach, strawberries, onion, cooked orzo pasta, and bacon bits in a large salad bowl. Pour the dressing over the salad, to taste, and toss until all ingredients are thoroughly mixed. Sprinkle the salad with the toasted pine nuts and feta cheese, if desired. Serve immediately. Makes approximately 6 servings.

Lavender Raspberry Vinaigrette

1/2 cup raspberries, fresh OR
   frozen
1/4 cup balsamic vinegar
1/4 cup white wine vinegar
2 tsp granulated sugar

1 Tbsp Dijon mustard
2 tsp Organic Culinary Lavender
   Buds
1/2 cup extra-virgin olive oil

Combine all of the ingredients, except for the oil, in a blender or food processor, and mix well. While mixing, slowly add the oil, a little at a time, until the dressing thickens and is well blended. This dressing is thicker than most vinaigrettes; if preferred, it can be thinned by simply adding more oil and vinegar to taste.

Photo Courtesy of Sandy & Wade Leonard

Recipe Tested in the Kitchen of Sandy & Wade Leonard

Creamy Garlic & Lavender Dressing

This dressing is incredibly simple to prepare and tastes just like the ones served by fine restaurants. It's superb on any garden or pasta salad; plus, it makes any ordinary side dish extraordinary. Try serving it over roasted red-skinned potatoes, steamed green beans, or baked asparagus. Add a little fresh-grated Parmesan cheese, and you've made a fabulous side dish!

1/4 tsp Organic Culinary Lavender Buds

1 1/2 cups light mayonnaise

2/3 cup light sour cream

1/4 cup red wine vinegar

1 Tbsp sugar

1/4 cup fresh-squeezed lemon juice

3 garlic cloves, minced

1/2 tsp fresh-ground black pepper

1/2 tsp salt

Grind the lavender buds in a spice grinder or coffee grinder. In a small mixing bowl, stir together all of the ingredients, and whisk until well blended. Cover, and chill for 2 hours before using. The dressing may be stored in the refrigerator for up to 2 weeks. Makes approximately 3 cups.

Chef's Comments

For a thinner dressing, add 1/4 cup of water when blending the ingredients.

Add 1/4 cup minced shallots or yellow onion for a little extra flavor and appeal.

Photo Courtesy of Nancy Feldbush

Recipe Tested in the Kitchen of Michelle & Richard Allen

Lavender Buttermilk Ranch Dressing

This lavender-infused version of the classic ranch dressing is terrific over a garden salad, and it's also a great tangy dip for fresh veggies and grilled chicken. The most wonderful thing about my Lavender Buttermilk Ranch Dressing is its freshness. It doesn't have all the preservatives that store-bought dressings contain—which makes it both healthier and more delicious.

2 Tbsp dried parsley

1 tsp dried dill

1/4 tsp dried minced onion

1/4 tsp dried minced garlic

1/4 tsp onion powder

1/4 tsp garlic powder

1/4 tsp salt

1/4 tsp fresh-ground black pepper

1/2 tsp Organic Culinary Lavender Buds

1 cup mayonnaise (we prefer Hellmann's brand)

3/4 cup buttermilk

In a small bowl, mix together all of the ingredients, except for the buttermilk. Slowly add the buttermilk while stirring constantly. Chill for at least 2 hours before serving. The dressing may be refrigerated for up to 1 week. Makes approximately 2 cups.

Chef's Comments

For a smoother dressing, add an additional 2 Tbsp of buttermilk.

To save time, premix several batches of the dried herbs, and store them in individual containers. The herbs will keep for quite a while, and they'll be ready—and premeasured—for making a batch of the dressing anytime.

For a more pronounced lavender taste, grind the lavender buds before adding them to the dressing.

Photos Courtesy of Nancy Feldbush

Recipe Tested in the Kitchen of Nancy Feldbush

Lavender Lane

Dinner Entrées

Mike's Classic Pasta Sauce with Lavender Garlic Meatballs

My husband has made this pasta sauce for years, and whenever we have company, Mike is usually seen mixing together his now-famous family favorite. If you are a garlic lover, the meatballs are sure to please your palate, and everything tastes even better the next day. This recipe makes a lot, but it freezes well for up to three months.

Meat Sauce

1/4 pound ground round

1 1/2 Tbsp olive oil

1 can (14.5 oz. size) tomato sauce (we prefer Hunt's brand)

1 can (14.5 oz. size) diced fire-roasted tomatoes (we prefer Hunt's brand)

1 can (14.5 oz. size) stewed tomatoes (we prefer Hunt's brand)

3 cans (12 oz. size) tomato paste (we prefer Contadina brand)

6 garlic cloves, minced

1/8 tsp salt

1/4 tsp fresh-ground black pepper

1 Tbsp dried sweet basil

2 tsp granulated sugar

6 cups water

3/4 cup Romano cheese

Meatballs

1/2 cup Italian bread crumbs (we prefer Progresso brand)

1/2 cup Romano cheese

1/8 tsp salt

1/4 tsp fresh-ground black pepper

1 tsp Organic Culinary Lavender Buds

1/2 tsp dried sweet basil

1/2 tsp dried oregano

1 1/2 pounds ground round

1 egg

10 garlic cloves, minced

1/2 cup water

pasta (use your favorite pasta, and make according to the package's directions)

In a large stockpot, brown the ground round in the olive oil. Strain the meat from the oil. Discard the oil, and set the meat aside. Combine all the remaining ingredients (in the meat sauce list) in the stockpot, and stir until smooth. Add the meat, and cook on medium-high heat until the sauce begins to bubble. Reduce the heat to low, and simmer the sauce, covering 3/4 of the pot with aluminum foil. Stir occasionally, and move around any tomatoes that may have settled on the bottom of the pot.

While the sauce is simmering, start the meatballs by combining the bread crumbs, cheese, salt, pepper, lavender buds, basil, and oregano in a small bowl. Mix until well blended, and set aside. In a separate, larger mixing bowl, thoroughly mix together the ground round, egg, and garlic. Add the bread crumb mixture one cup at a time, and blend well after each addition. It is important that the spices are distributed evenly because they will have a major effect on the consistency and flavor in the final product. Next, add the water, a little bit at a time, and mix until well incorporated. Form 2-inch meatballs (about 24), being certain to pack each tightly in order to make firm meatballs.

Chef's Comments

There's no need to be overly fussy about the sauce while it's cooking, but it is recommended that you gently stir the sauce with a large spoon every 15 minutes to prevent any burning. When stirring, move around any items that may have settled on the bottom and bring them to the top. Use care not to break any of the meatballs. Gently pat down the meatballs after mixing so they're immersed within the sauce.

Place the meatballs in the sauce one by one, and gently stir. Re-cover 3/4 of the pot with the aluminum foil. Simmer the meatballs in the sauce for about 2 hours or until the meatballs are cooked completely. Serve over your favorite pasta. Complete this tasty meal with the Herbal Butter Garlic Bread found on page 199. Makes approximately 8–10 servings.

Recipe Tested in the Kitchen of Linda Mascagni

Fettuccine with Lavender Garlic Alfredo

Surprisingly simple to prepare, Alfredo sauce is a masterpiece of Italian cuisine. This recipe comes from my sister Sharon, who tends to just "throw" ingredients together when cooking, but it always works for her because her meals are amazing. And, of course, I had to add a touch of lavender, which takes this rich and decadent sauce to a whole new level of flavor.

1 pound uncooked fettuccine pasta

6 Tbsp butter

2–3 garlic cloves, minced

1 1/2 cups heavy whipping cream

1/2 cup fresh-grated Parmesan cheese

sea salt (to taste)

fresh-ground black pepper (to taste)

1/4 tsp Organic Culinary Lavender Buds

1/4 cup fresh parsley, chopped (for garnish—optional)

Cook the pasta according to the package's directions, and drain. In a large skillet, heat the butter over very low heat, and sauté the garlic for about 2 minutes. Add the whipping cream, increase the heat to medium-low, and continue to cook for 4–5 minutes until the amount of the cream reduces slightly. Add the Parmesan cheese, salt, pepper, and lavender buds. Stir well. Add the pasta to the sauce. Toss the fettuccine in the sauce until it is well coated. Serve immediately, and garnish with chopped fresh parsley, if desired. Makes approximately 6–8 servings.

Variation

Add grilled chicken or steak or your favorite steamed vegetables, such as broccoli, carrots, and zucchini, to make this pasta even more filling.

Photo Courtesy of Julie Kampling

Recipe Tested in the Kitchen of Julie Kampling

Zucchini Eggplant Lasagna with Lavender, Tomato & Basil

This lasagna is impressive and offers a wonderful vegetarian alternative to the traditional meaty version. The lavender and basil add an enticing flavor to the filling, and the vegetables are absolutely magnificent! Serve it with your favorite garlic bread (or make the recipe on page 199) and a mixed-green salad, and you've got a meal that is sure to dazzle.

21 lasagna noodles

1 Tbsp olive oil, plus 1 Tbsp, separated

1 cup zucchini, finely chopped (about 1 medium)

1 cup eggplant, finely chopped (about 1 small)

1 cup carrots, finely chopped (about 3 medium)

1/2 cup yellow onion, minced (about 1 small)

1/2 cup orange bell pepper, finely chopped

1/2 cup Roma tomatoes, thinly sliced

5 garlic cloves, minced

1 Tbsp butter

1 pkg (8 oz. size) sliced mushrooms

1 pkg (6 oz. size) baby spinach leaves, thinly sliced

1 container (15 oz. size) ricotta cheese

2 eggs, well-beaten

3 cups shredded Italian cheese blend (we prefer Kraft brand)

1 cup fresh-grated Parmesan cheese

1/2 tsp sea salt

1/4 tsp fresh-ground black pepper

2 Tbsp fresh basil, chopped

1 Tbsp Organic Culinary Lavender Buds

1 tsp dried rosemary

2 jars (24 oz. size) tomato and basil pasta sauce (we prefer Bertolli brand)

1/2 cup Fontina cheese (used for the top of the lasagna)

Cook the lasagna noodles according to the package's directions. Drain, rinse with cold water, and drain again. Set aside.

In a large skillet, heat 1 Tbsp of the olive oil over medium-high heat. Add the zucchini, eggplant, carrots, onion, bell pepper, tomatoes, and garlic. Sauté over medium-low heat for about 5 minutes or until the vegetables are slightly tender. Transfer the vegetables to a bowl, and set aside. Heat the remaining 1 Tbsp of olive oil and the butter in the skillet, and sauté the mushrooms over medium-low heat for 5 minutes or until tender. Gradually add the spinach, and cook for an additional 2 minutes or until the spinach is wilted. Add the spinach and mushrooms to the other vegetables, and toss. Set aside. In a medium-size mixing bowl, combine the ricotta cheese, eggs, Italian cheese blend, Parmesan cheese, salt, pepper, basil, lavender buds, and rosemary, and mix well. Set aside.

Preheat the oven to 375°F. To assemble the lasagna, spread 1 cup of the pasta sauce in the bottom of a 9-inch x 13-inch baking dish. Arrange one layer of the noodles in the bottom of the pan, overlapping as necessary to completely cover the bottom. Top with 1/3 of the vegetable mixture. Spoon 1/3 of the cheese mixture over the vegetables, and spread evenly. Add 1/4 of the pasta sauce. Add another layer of noodles, overlapping as necessary to completely cover the filling, and repeat the steps for adding the vegetables, cheeses, and sauce. Make another layer, repeating the above steps. All of the vegetable and cheese mixtures should now be gone. Top the lasagna with a final layer of noodles, and spread the remaining pasta sauce on top of the noodles. Gently "pack down" the lasagna using the back of a spatula.

Place the lasagna on a foil-lined baking sheet, such as a cookie sheet. This will protect your oven just in case the lasagna bubbles over a bit. Bake at 375° for about 45 minutes. Add the 1/2 cup of Fontina cheese, and return the lasagna to the oven. Bake for an additional 15 minutes or until heated through. Let stand 10–15 minutes before serving. Makes approximately 6 servings.

Recipe Tested in the Kitchen of Tony Kampling

Southwest Lavender Chicken Enchiladas

This easy-to-prepare recipe is a variation of my famous sour cream chicken enchiladas. The ingredients are layered in a baking dish like lasagna, which allows the flavors to blend together beautifully. This dish is even better when served with your favorite black beans, rice, and salsa.

1 Tbsp olive oil

2 Tbsp butter

1 medium Vidalia onion OR other sweet onion, minced

1 garlic clove, minced

1/4 cup fresh-squeezed lemon juice

2 pounds boneless, skinless chicken breasts, thinly sliced

2 tsp Organic Culinary Lavender Buds

1 tsp sea salt

2 tsp fresh-ground black pepper

1 tsp ground cumin

1 can (10.75 oz. size) cream of chicken soup

1/4 cup whole milk, plus 2 Tbsp, separated

1 container (8 oz. size) sour cream

1 can (14.5 oz. size) diced tomatoes with green chilies

1 pkg (16 oz. size) whole wheat tortillas, cut in half

4 corn tortillas, cut in half

1 pkg (8 oz. size) shredded Mexican cheese blend

In a medium-size frying pan, heat the olive oil and butter over medium heat, and sauté the onion and garlic for 3–4 minutes. Add the lemon juice and chicken slices. Sprinkle the lavender buds, salt, pepper, and cumin over the chicken. Cook on low heat, covered, until the chicken is tender, about 12–16 minutes. Remove from the heat, and allow the chicken to cool in the pan.

In a medium-size mixing bowl, add the soup, the 1/4 cup of milk, and the sour cream. Mix well. Remove 2 Tbsp of this sauce mixture, place in a small container, and set aside (it will be used later). Add the diced tomatoes with green chilies to the mixing bowl, and stir well. Once the chicken is cooled, drain any liquid from the pan, but make sure to keep the onion and garlic pieces in the pan. Shred the chicken with a fork. Mix the shredded chicken together with the remaining ingredients in the frying pan.

Preheat the oven to 350°F. In a 9-inch x 13-inch glass baking dish, put a spoonful of the tomato sauce mixture in the bottom of the pan, and spread evenly. Place a single layer of the wheat tortillas over the tomato sauce mixture on the bottom of the baking dish. Now, place a layer of the corn tortillas on top of the wheat tortillas. Then spread half of the shredded chicken, half of the tomato sauce mixture, and half of the shredded cheese on top of the tortillas. Layer it just as you would when making lasagna. Repeat. Cover all of the ingredients in the baking dish with a single layer of wheat tortillas.

In a small saucepan, combine the 2 Tbsp of milk and the 2 Tbsp of the sauce mixture that was set aside earlier. Heat on low, and mix until smooth. Pour this sauce over the top of the wheat tortillas, spreading evenly. Cover the baking dish with aluminum foil, and bake at 350° for 50–60 minutes or until the enchiladas begin to bubble on the side of the baking dish. Serve with black beans, rice, and salsa. Makes approximately 4–6 servings.

Recipe Tested in the Kitchen of Tony Kampling

Lavender Chicken Florentine Stuffed Shells

Always a family favorite, this pasta dish blends together savory Italian cheeses with spinach, garlic, and lavender-roasted chicken. When I make these shells for company, I keep the lavender a secret until my guests have devoured every tidbit and raved about the delicious meal. By then, the lavender has won over even the toughest skeptic!

2 boneless, skinless chicken breasts

1 lemon

1 Tbsp Organic Culinary Lavender Buds

1 container (24 oz. size) ricotta cheese

2 egg yolks

4 garlic cloves, minced

1 small yellow onion, minced

2 tsp dried basil

2 tsp dried oregano

2 tsp dried parsley

1 tsp sea salt

2 tsp fresh-ground black pepper

2 cups baby spinach leaves, minced

2/3 cup asiago cheese, shredded

1 pkg (8 oz. size) shredded Italian cheese blend (we prefer Kraft brand)

2/3 cup fresh-grated Parmesan cheese

18–22 large uncooked pasta shells

2 jars (24 oz. size) tomato and basil pasta sauce (we prefer Bertolli brand)

Variation

This recipe can be easily converted into a meatless version— without losing any of the flavor! Simply omit the chicken and lemon, and reduce the amount of lavender buds from 1 Tbsp to 2 tsp. Add the 2 tsp of lavender buds to the cheese filling.

Preheat the oven to 375°F. Place the chicken breasts in a small roasting pan. Squeeze the juice from the lemon over the chicken, and then sprinkle with the lavender buds. Cover, and bake at 375° for 25 minutes or until the chicken is done. Remove from the oven, and allow to cool.

In a mixing bowl, blend together the ricotta cheese and egg yolks until smooth. Add the garlic, onion, basil, oregano, parsley, salt, and pepper. Mix well. Fold in the spinach, asiago cheese, and cheese blend along with half of the Parmesan cheese. Set aside the other half of the Parmesan cheese for later use. In a large pot, boil enough water to cook the pasta shells. Cook according to the package's directions, rinse with cold water, and set aside.

Shred the chicken, and add it to the cheese mixture, blending well. Spread 2 cups of the pasta sauce in an 11-inch x 17-inch baking dish to prevent the pasta shells from sticking to the pan while baking.

Spoon about 3 heaping Tbsp of the chicken and cheese filling into each cooked pasta shell, and place the shells into the baking dish. Line the shells closely together until you fill the baking dish. Spoon any remaining filling over the shells. Evenly distribute the remaining pasta sauce over the shells.

Bake, uncovered, at 375° for 35–45 minutes or until the sauce begins to bubble. Sprinkle the shells with the remaining Parmesan cheese, and serve. Makes approximately 6 servings.

Recipe Tested in the Kitchen of David Stockton

Grilled Pineapple Chicken with Lavender Honey Glaze

Ideal for any summertime meal, this grilled chicken has a sweet kick of honey; plus, the pineapple and the lavender glaze make every bite amazing. My family prefers this chicken served with seasoned vegetables and wild rice, but it's so versatile that it goes with practically anything, including salads.

Lavender Honey Glaze

2 Tbsp butter

2 garlic cloves, finely minced

1/3 cup fresh-squeezed lime juice

1/2 cup honey

3 Tbsp soy sauce

1 Tbsp Organic Culinary Lavender Buds

1/2 tsp ground ginger

Chicken

6 boneless, skinless chicken breast halves

6 pineapple rings

To make the Lavender Honey Glaze, in a skillet, heat the butter over medium heat, and sauté the garlic for 1–2 minutes. Whisk in the lime juice, honey, soy sauce, lavender buds, and ground ginger. Remove from the heat. Divide the glaze in half.

Place the chicken breasts in a covered container with half of the Lavender Honey Glaze, and allow it to marinate, in the refrigerator, for at least 1 hour. Set aside the other half of the glaze for basting when grilling.

Lightly oil a gas, charcoal, or electric grill. Place the chicken on the grill, and cook for 6–8 minutes per side, basting with the reserved Lavender Honey Glaze every few minutes. The chicken is done when the meat is firm and when the juices run clear after being pierced with a fork.

Place the pineapple rings on the grill, and baste with the remaining Lavender Honey Glaze. Cook just until the pineapple develops a grill mark, and then turn over. Continue basting with the glaze, and cook the rings for another 3–4 minutes.

Place the chicken on a serving plate, and top with the grilled pineapple. Serve with your favorite seasoned vegetables and wild rice, if desired. Makes approximately 6 servings.

Photo Courtesy of Richard Allen

Recipe Tested in the Kitchen of Michelle & Richard Allen

Lavender Chicken Scaloppine with Lemon Butter Sauce

This dish makes up quite easily and is absolutely scrumptious. The capers and prosciutto add a light salty taste, which perfectly complements the rest of the ingredients. Mamma Mia!

Lemon Butter Sauce

1/2 cup fresh-squeezed lemon juice

1/4 cup chicken broth (for best taste, use broth from a carton, instead of a can)

1/4 cup white wine

1/4 cup light cream

1 stick unsalted butter, cubed

1/2 tsp fresh-ground black pepper

Chicken Scaloppine

3 Tbsp olive oil

2 garlic cloves, minced

1 1/2 pounds boneless, skinless chicken breasts, thinly sliced

1 tsp Organic Culinary Lavender Buds

1 pkg (12 oz. size) sliced mushrooms

4 oz. prosciutto, cut into strips

1 can (12 oz. size) marinated artichoke hearts, drained and sliced

2 Tbsp capers

1 pound uncooked angel hair pasta

fresh parsley and fresh-grated Parmesan cheese (for garnish)

Chef's Comments

For an even creamier sauce, use heavy whipping cream instead of the light cream.

Prosciutto is a spiced Italian ham and can be found at an Italian market or gourmet food store.

To make the Lemon Butter Sauce, combine the lemon juice, chicken broth, and white wine in a medium-size saucepan. Bring the mixture to a boil, and allow it to cook until it is about 1/3 the amount you started with. Reduce the heat, and slowly add the cream. Simmer, stirring constantly, for about 4 minutes or until the mixture begins to thicken. Add the butter, and stir until it is completely melted. Sprinkle with the pepper. Remove from the heat, cover, and set aside.

In a large skillet, heat the olive oil over medium heat, and sauté the garlic for about 1–2 minutes. Add the chicken to the pan, and sprinkle it with the lavender buds. Cover, and cook over medium heat, turning once, about 5–8 minutes or until the chicken is almost done. Add the mushrooms and prosciutto to the chicken, and continue to cook until the mushrooms and chicken are fully cooked, about another 5–8 minutes. Add the artichoke hearts and capers, and toss together with the Lemon Butter Sauce. Heat for an additional 2–3 minutes.

Photo Courtesy of Doreen Weisgerber

While the chicken is cooking, make the pasta according to the package's directions, and drain. Serve the chicken and lemon butter mixture over the cooked pasta. Garnish with fresh parsley and fresh-grated Parmesan cheese. Makes approximately 6 servings.

Recipe Tested in the Kitchen of Doreen Weisgerber

Provençal Meat Loaf

When you are looking for something fast and fabulous, this meat loaf is sure to do the trick! Inspired by the taste of my Lavender Lemon Pepper seasoning, my sister Jan threw this meat loaf together one night for dinner, and ever since then, she has had requests to make it over and over again. It is best when made with ground lamb; although, ground turkey is an excellent substitute.

Meat Loaf

1 pound ground lamb OR ground turkey

1 tsp Lavender Lemon Pepper (see the recipe on page 18)

1/2 tsp dried rosemary

1 large egg, beaten

2 garlic cloves, finely minced

1 cup organic rolled oats

1/2 medium onion, finely minced

Garnish

1/2 medium onion, thinly sliced

2 Tbsp olive oil

1/2 tsp Lavender Lemon Pepper

Preheat the oven to 350°F.

In a large mixing bowl, combine together the ground meat, Lavender Lemon Pepper, and rosemary until the seasonings are well distributed throughout the meat.

Add the remaining ingredients for the meat loaf, and mix thoroughly, by hand, until all of the ingredients are well blended.

Form the meat mixture into an 8-inch x 3-inch rectangular loaf. Place the loaf on a baking sheet lined with parchment paper.

Garnish the loaf with the thin slices of onion, brush with the olive oil, and sprinkle with the 1/2 tsp of Lavender Lemon Pepper.

Bake at 350° for 30 minutes or until the center is no longer pink. Makes approximately 4 servings.

Variation

Add 1/2 cup finely chopped fresh spinach or 1/2 cup finely chopped mushrooms for extra flavor and appeal.

Recipe Tested in the Kitchen of Christina Schultz

Baked Orange Roughy with Lavender Citrus Glaze

Both healthful and bursting with flavor, my Baked Orange Roughy with Lavender Citrus Glaze is delightfully appetizing and very simple to prepare. I usually serve it with wild rice and steamed vegetables, but it's great with just about anything!

Lavender Citrus Glaze (see the recipe on the next page)

1 1/2 pounds orange roughy fillets

2 Tbsp butter, melted

1/4 cup fresh-squeezed lemon juice

1 Tbsp fresh parsley, minced OR 2 tsp dried parsley

1/2 tsp sea salt

1/4 tsp fresh-ground black pepper

sliced almonds (for garnish—optional)

Preheat the oven to 350°F. Prepare the Lavender Citrus Glaze, and set aside.

In a shallow baking dish, arrange the fish fillets in a single layer. Combine the melted butter with the lemon juice, and pour over the fish. Sprinkle with the parsley, salt, and pepper. Cover, and bake at 350° for 10 minutes.

After the fish has baked for the 10 minutes, remove it from the oven. Spoon half of the Lavender Citrus Glaze over the fish. Return the fish to the oven, and bake, uncovered, for an additional 10 minutes.

To check if the fish is done, use the tip of a sharp knife or a fork to cut through the center of the fillets; the fish will easily flake when finished cooking. Bake for an additional 4–5 minutes, if necessary.

Top the fish fillets with the remaining Lavender Citrus Glaze. If you prefer, sliced almonds can be added over the glaze. Makes approximately 6 servings.

Lavender Citrus Glaze

1/3 cup orange marmalade	1 garlic clove, finely minced
1/3 cup honey	1/2 tsp Organic Culinary Lavender
1/3 cup orange juice	Buds

In a small saucepan, mix together all of the ingredients, and bring the mixture to a boil over medium-high heat. Reduce the heat to low. Stirring occasionally, simmer the glaze, uncovered, for 15–20 minutes or until it is slightly thickened.

Recipe Tested in the Kitchen of Doreen Weisgerber

Lavender Grilled Salmon with Herb-Seasoned Vegetables

This recipe for Lavender Grilled Salmon is a spectacular creation by Victoria Connolly, owner of Victoria's Delights in downtown Oxford, Michigan. Victoria's restaurant has catered our annual Michigan Lavender Festival for years, and her fresh and healthy bistro-to-go menu is something that everyone looks forward to with great anticipation. My favorite accompaniment to her grilled salmon is fresh, Herb-Seasoned Vegetables— which makes an unbeatable combo.

4 Tbsp honey

6 Tbsp olive oil

1/2 tsp Organic Culinary
   Lavender Buds, chopped

1/4 cup white wine

1 Tbsp Worcestershire sauce

1 tsp fresh-squeezed lemon juice

3 pounds salmon fillets

sea salt (to taste)

fresh-ground black pepper (to taste)

Herb-Seasoned Vegetables (see the recipe on the next page)

Photo Courtesy of Valerie Harms

Combine together the honey, olive oil, lavender buds, wine, Worcestershire sauce, and lemon juice in a small saucepan. Stirring constantly with a wire whisk, cook the mixture over medium heat until it is about 2/3 the amount you started with. Remove the sauce from the heat, and set aside to cool.

Season the salmon fillets with the salt and pepper. When the sauce has cooled slightly, brush some of it on the salmon fillets.

Lightly oil a gas, charcoal, or electric grill. Grill the salmon, basting with the sauce every few minutes. However, do not use all of the sauce for basting; set a little aside for a finishing touch. When the salmon easily flakes or when the internal temperature of the fish reaches 150°F on a meat thermometer, it is ready. Top the fillets with the remaining sauce, and serve with Herb-Seasoned Vegetables. Makes approximately 6–8 servings.

Herb-Seasoned Vegetables

2 Tbsp butter

1 cup carrots, thinly sliced

1/2 small yellow onion, cubed

1 cup red bell pepper, thinly sliced

1 pkg (9–10 oz. size) frozen
asparagus, thawed and drained

1/2 tsp dried thyme

sea salt (to taste)

fresh-ground black pepper (to taste)

In a medium-size skillet, heat the butter over medium heat, and sauté the carrots, onion, and pepper until the carrots are slightly tender, about 5 minutes. Add the asparagus and thyme, and continue to cook until the asparagus is heated through. Sprinkle with salt and pepper, and serve with the Lavender Grilled Salmon. Makes approximately 6 servings.

Recipe Tested in the Kitchen of Valerie Harms

Lavender Roasted Leg of Lamb

This recipe is from my sister Jan, who is an excellent cook. She has a fondness for dishes that are simple to prepare yet full of flavor—and her Lavender Roasted Leg of Lamb fits both of those requirements to a T.

2 Tbsp extra-virgin olive oil

1 medium onion, thinly sliced

2 garlic cloves, minced

2–3 pounds boneless leg of lamb

1 Tbsp Organic Culinary Lavender Buds

sea salt & fresh-ground black pepper (to taste)

1 cup water

2 cups Brussels sprouts

6–8 small red-skinned potatoes, washed and quartered

2 cups baby carrots

2 Tbsp fresh parsley, chopped (for garnish—optional)

2 Tbsp red bell pepper, finely diced (for garnish—optional)

Preheat the oven to 275°F.

In a large skillet, heat the olive oil over medium heat, and sauté the onion and garlic for about 4 minutes. Add the lamb, and sprinkle it with the lavender buds and the salt and pepper, to taste. Brown the lamb for about 5–7 minutes on each side.

Place the browned lamb and onion mixture in a glass baking dish. Add the water, cover, and bake at 275° for 1 hour and 20 minutes.

Increase the oven temperature to 350°F, and add the Brussels sprouts, potatoes, and carrots. Cover, and bake at 350° for 1 more hour. Garnish, and serve. Makes approximately 4–6 servings.

Chef's Comments

A great way to present this dish is to sprinkle the outside of a serving platter with a confetti of chopped fresh parsley and finely diced red bell pepper, then add the lamb and vegetables.

Years ago, my husband bought me an unusual gift, which has since become a treasure in our kitchen: a garlic press! This tool minces the garlic quickly and effortlessly, saving you from peeling and mincing the garlic by hand. This handy tool can be found at gourmet markets or online, and I highly recommend that every cook have one.

Recipe Tested in the Kitchen of Tony Kampling

Provençal Beef with Vegetables

When your friends and family taste this flavorful dish, they'll think you spent all day in the kitchen preparing it, but only you will know the truth— it can be made in about half an hour using just a skillet. Enjoy!

2 Tbsp butter

1 pound boneless beef tip steak, cut into thin strips

1 cup pearl onions, cut in half

1/8 tsp sea salt

1 1/2 tsp Herbs de Provence (with lavender)

3 cups red-skinned potatoes, washed and thinly sliced

1 cup carrots, thinly sliced

1 cup broccoli, cut into bite-size pieces

2 cups frozen cut green beans

1 tsp Worcestershire sauce

3/4 cup beef broth

1/4 cup cold water

1 Tbsp cornstarch

Melt the butter in a large nonstick skillet over medium-high heat. Add the beef and onions to the skillet, and sprinkle with the salt and Herbs de Provence.

Chef's Comments

Herbs de Provence can be purchased at most specialty stores or online at www.AllThingsLavender.com.

You can also create your own Herbs de Provence by following the recipe on page 19.

Cook and stir until the beef is browned. Transfer the beef mixture to a bowl, and set aside. Cover the beef to keep it warm.

In the same skillet, combine the remaining ingredients (except for the water and cornstarch), and bring them to a boil. Reduce the heat to medium, cover the skillet, and simmer the vegetables, stirring occasionally, for about 15 minutes or until the potatoes are tender.

In the meantime, in a small bowl, combine the water and cornstarch, and stir until smooth. Add the beef to the cooked vegetables along with the cornstarch, and stir well. Cook until the mixture becomes bubbly and the sauce thickens, about 5–7 minutes. Makes approximately 4 servings.

Photo Courtesy of Julie Kampling

Recipe Tested in the Kitchen of Julie Kampling

Lavender Lane

Breads,
Muffins
& Scones

Herbal Butter

From savory to sweet to soothing, this simple recipe offers hundreds of flavorful possibilities.

1 stick unsalted butter

1 tsp fresh-squeezed lemon juice

2–3 Tbsp fresh herbs, chopped (lavender buds, chives, parsley, tarragon, and
rosemary all work wonderfully)

Soften the butter. Cream together the butter, lemon juice, and herbs. Mix until well blended. Place in a container, and refrigerate. Store in the refrigerator up to a week or in the freezer for a month. Makes approximately 1/2 cup.

Chef's Comments

Use any combination of your favorite herbs for a tasty treat.

Our favorite combinations are...

lavender and rosemary

lavender and chives

lavender, thyme, and parsley

Photos Courtesy of Nancy Feldbush

Variation

For an excellent garlic bread, try this recipe for Herbal Butter Garlic Bread.

Make the Herbal Butter recipe, and use 2 cloves of minced garlic, lavender buds, thyme, and parsley as the fresh herbs. Spread the butter over french bread, and sprinkle with fresh-grated Parmesan cheese. Bake at 425°F until golden brown.

Recipe Tested in the Kitchen of Nancy Feldbush

Grandma's Cheddar & Herb Buttermilk Biscuits

This delicious biscuit is flavored with cheddar, garlic, buttermilk, and Herbs de Provence. And, with one bite, it'll feel—and taste—as if you were in a countryside café in Provence.

2 cups all-purpose flour

1 tsp sea salt

1/4 tsp baking soda

1 Tbsp baking powder

6 Tbsp unsalted butter, very cold, cut into cubes

1/2 cup cheddar cheese, shredded

2 tsp Herbs de Provence (with lavender)

3/4 cup buttermilk, very cold

Baked Biscuits Topping

1/4 cup melted butter

1/2 tsp garlic powder

Chef's Comments

Herbs de Provence can be purchased at most specialty stores or online at www.AllThingsLavender.com.

You can also create your own Herbs de Provence by following the recipe on page 19.

Preheat the oven to 450°F. Mix together the flour, salt, baking soda, and baking powder in a food processor or large mixing bowl. Add the butter to the flour mixture. Pulse in a food processor or cut in with a pastry blender until the mixture resembles a coarse meal. Add the cheese and Herbs de Provence, and pulse (or mix) well. Being careful not to over-mix, add the buttermilk, just until the ingredients combine. If the dough seems a little dry, add a tiny bit more buttermilk, and mix very lightly.

Turn the dough onto a lightly floured surface. *Gently* pat the dough to about a 1/2-inch thickness. (Do not roll or over-work the dough.) Use a round cutter to cut the dough into biscuits. Gently knead together the scraps to make a few more biscuits, again using care not to over-work the dough. Place the biscuits on a nonstick baking sheet about 1 inch apart. Bake at 450° for 10–12 minutes or until they are golden brown on top. Do not over-bake.

While the biscuits are baking, stir together the melted butter and garlic powder; brush over the finished biscuits before removing them from the baking sheet. Serve warm. Makes approximately 12 biscuits.

Photo Courtesy of Julie Kampling

Chef's Comments

The secret to perfect biscuits is in the proper handling of the dough.

When mixing the dough, handle it as little as possible; otherwise, you will have tough biscuits.

A food processor is the greatest tool for producing great biscuits every time. The ingredients stay colder, and there's less chance of over-working the dough.

Recipe Tested in the Kitchen of Julie Kampling

Lavender Focaccia Bread

A type of flat bread, focaccia bread was probably an early prototype of today's pizza crust. This savory bread is simple to make and perfect for your next party because it can be prepared a day ahead. Simply prepare, refrigerate, and then bake the day of the festivities.

1 loaf (1 pound size) frozen bread dough

1 Tbsp extra-virgin olive oil, plus 1 Tbsp, separated

1 small red onion, thinly sliced

2 garlic cloves, minced

1 tsp Organic Culinary Lavender Buds

1 tsp dried rosemary

1/2 tsp dried oregano

1/4 cup black olives, sliced

1/3 cup feta cheese, crumbled

Thaw the bread dough according to the package's directions. Preheat the oven to 375°F.

Roll the dough into a 10-inch x 14-inch rectangle, and place it on a nonstick cookie sheet. Brush with 1 Tbsp of the olive oil.

In a skillet, heat the other 1 Tbsp of olive oil over medium heat, and sauté the onion and garlic for about 2 minutes or until the onion is softened. Evenly spread the cooked onion and garlic over the bread dough. Sprinkle the top with the herbs, black olives, and crumbled feta cheese.

Bake at 375° for 20–25 minutes or until the bread is golden brown. Cool for 3–4 minutes, and cut into small rectangles. Serve with your favorite pasta, soup, or salad. Makes approximately 4 side-dish-size servings or 12 hors d'oeuvre-size servings.

Variation

Try adding seasonal fresh vegetables, such as thinly sliced tomatoes, zucchini, or eggplant, for a wonderful vegetarian pizza.

Photo Courtesy of Julie Kampling

Recipe Tested in the Kitchen of Julie Kampling

Lavender Olive Bread with Rosemary & Parmesan Bread Dipper

When you bite into a piece of this aromatic olive bread, you'll think you're vacationing somewhere in the Mediterranean. And, when served with my Rosemary & Parmesan Bread Dipper (see the recipe on the next page), it's completely irresistible. The leftovers, if there are any, make a delectable bread to use for sandwiches.

1 Tbsp quick active dry yeast

1 Tbsp granulated sugar

1 cup very warm water

1 1/2 cups all-purpose flour

1 cup whole wheat flour

2 Tbsp melted butter

1/2 cup Sicilian olives, pitted and sliced

1/2 cup kalamata olives, pitted and sliced

1 1/2 tsp Organic Culinary Lavender Buds

1 Tbsp fresh rosemary, chopped OR 1 1/2 tsp dried rosemary

2 tsp fresh thyme, chopped OR 1/2 tsp dried thyme

2 tsp olive oil (for garnish—optional)

2 tsp sea salt (for garnish—optional)

In a large bowl, mix together the yeast, sugar, and water, and allow it to bubble for about 5 minutes. Add the remaining ingredients. Mix by hand or in a food processor until the dough is smooth and elastic. If the dough is too sticky, add 1 or 2 Tbsp more flour as needed to make the dough easy to handle. It should not be too wet or too dry.

Place the dough on a lightly floured surface, and knead for about 10 minutes, folding over and turning frequently, until the dough is smooth and springs up when you push on it. Rub olive oil on the inside of a large mixing bowl. Place the dough into the bowl, cover it with a towel, and place it in a warm area for about 1 hour or until it doubles in size. The dough is ready if an indentation remains when you touch it.

Oil a cookie sheet using olive oil, and sprinkle it with a touch of sea salt, if desired. Gently punch down the dough to deflate it. Divide the dough in half, and form it into 2 small rounded loaves. Evenly space the loaves on the cookie sheet, allowing them enough room to double in size. Let the loaves rise again in a warm place for about 45 minutes or until they double in size.

Preheat the oven to 375°F. Move the oven rack to the middle of the oven. Bake at 375° for 15–20 minutes or until the bread is light golden brown and sounds hollow when tapped. Carefully remove the loaves from the oven. Garnish the bread with olive oil, and sprinkle with sea salt, if desired. Cool slightly. Slice with a serrated bread knife, and serve with the Rosemary & Parmesan Bread Dipper (see the recipe below). Makes 2 loaves.

Rosemary & Parmesan Bread Dipper

3/4 cup extra-virgin olive oil
2 tsp fresh rosemary, chopped OR 1 tsp dried
    rosemary
1/3 cup fresh-grated Parmesan cheese
1 Tbsp balsamic vinegar
2 tsp fresh-ground black pepper

Place all the ingredients in a small bowl, and mix well. Serve with warm bread.

Chef's Comments

To give the bread a nice, crisp, golden brown finish, brush the tops of the loaves with a slightly beaten egg white halfway through the baking time. When brushing on the egg white, be very gentle so the bread does not fall.

Recipe Tested in the Kitchen of Jan Wiley

Whole Wheat Bread with Lavender Honey Butter

While growing up, I treasured our family get-togethers, and one of my favorite memories of those gatherings was my sister Sharon's Whole Wheat Bread. She would always make this bountiful treat and serve it with honey butter. It made our get-togethers complete. I couldn't help but add my usual signature to Sharon's trademark specialty—the hint of lavender adds wonderful appeal to this already delicious combination.

1 1/2 cups whole wheat flour

2 1/2 Tbsp Lavender Honey (see page 17 for the recipe)

1 Tbsp butter-flavored shortening

1/2 Tbsp salt

1 pkg (1/4 oz. size) quick active dry yeast

1 cup plus 1 Tbsp very warm water

1 1/2–2 cups all-purpose flour

1 Tbsp melted butter

Lavender Honey Butter (see the next page)

Variation

To make rolls, divide the dough into 12 pieces. Instead of putting the bread on a cookie sheet, place the dough into a well-greased, 12-cup muffin pan. Decrease the baking time to 20–25 minutes.

In a large bowl, mix together the whole wheat flour, honey, shortening, salt, and yeast. Add the warm water, and beat with an electric mixer on low speed for 1 minute. Scrape the sides of the bowl as necessary. Stir in enough of the all-purpose flour, adding a little at a time, to make the dough easy to handle. It should not be too wet or too dry. Place the dough on a lightly floured surface, and knead for about 10 minutes, folding over and turning frequently, until the dough is smooth and springs up when you push on it. Grease the inside of a large mixing bowl. Place the dough into the bowl, cover it with plastic wrap, and place it in a warm area for about 45–60 minutes or until it doubles in size. The dough is ready if an indentation remains when you touch it.

Gently punch down the dough to deflate it. Dust your working surface with some wheat flour, and place the dough on it. Flatten the dough with your hand or a rolling pin to create a 9-inch x 18-inch rectangle. Roll the dough up tightly, beginning at the 9-inch side. As you roll, pinch together the edges of the "pinwheel" ends—this seals the ends and keeps the dough from unrolling. Fold the ends under the loaf. Grease a cookie sheet, and place the loaf, seam side down, on the sheet. Lightly brush the loaf with melted butter, and loosely cover with plastic wrap. Allow the bread to rise in a warm place for about 20–45 minutes or until it doubles in size.

Preheat the oven to 375°F. Position your oven rack so the top of the bread will be in the center of the oven. Bake at 375° for 35–45 minutes or until the bread is golden brown and sounds hollow when tapped. Remove from the oven, and brush with more melted butter. Cool, slice, and serve with Lavender Honey Butter. Makes 1 loaf.

Lavender Honey Butter

2 sticks butter, softened
1/4 cup honey
1 tsp Organic Culinary
    Lavender Buds

In a medium-size mixing bowl, whip together the ingredients until light and fluffy. Remove the butter from the bowl, and spoon onto parchment paper or plastic wrap. Form into a log, and refrigerate for 2 hours before using. Store the Lavender Honey Butter in an airtight container, and refrigerate for up to 2 weeks. Makes approximately 1 cup. To make the Lavender Honey Butter without the lavender buds in the finished product, see the "Chef's" box on page 57.

Recipe Tested in the Kitchen of Barbara Parr

Lavender Honey Zucchini Bread

I have always been intrigued by honey-based recipes, which use honey instead of granulated sugar. Inspired by the possibilities, I revised my zucchini bread recipe so that it uses only honey as a sweetener. That change—along with the addition of carrots and raisins—makes this bread chock-full of goodness, and the Lavender Honey gives just a subtle hint of the herb and blends superbly with the other spices.

1 egg

3/4 cup Lavender Honey (see page 17 for the recipe)

3 Tbsp vegetable oil

1 tsp orange extract

1/4 tsp cinnamon

2 1/2 cups all-purpose flour

1 1/2 tsp baking powder

1/2 tsp baking soda

1/2 tsp ground ginger

1/4 tsp sea salt

1 1/2 cups zucchini, grated

1/2 cup carrots, grated

1/4 cup raisins

1/2 cup walnuts, finely chopped

Chef's Comments

Since this bread uses Lavender Honey as both a flavoring and a sweetener, the lavender taste is quite delicate. If you desire a more predominate lavender flavor, try topping the bread with Lavender Vanilla Icing, which can be found on page 45.

Preheat the oven to 350°F. In a large bowl, beat together the egg, honey, oil, orange extract, and cinnamon. In a separate bowl, combine the flour and remaining ingredients, and mix thoroughly. Gradually add the flour mixture to the honey mixture, stirring until all ingredients are well blended.

Spoon the batter into a well-greased 9-inch x 5-inch x 3-inch loaf pan. Bake at 350° for about 1 hour or until a toothpick inserted in the center comes out clean. Cool 10 minutes in the pan. Remove from the pan, and cool completely before serving. Serve with a drizzle of Lavender Honey, if desired. Makes 1 loaf.

Photo Courtesy of Debbie Walter

Recipe Tested in the Kitchen of Debbie Walter

Orange Lavender Poppy Seed Muffins

These moist muffins are an absolute treasure. They make teatime more enjoyable and are wonderful served plain or with the Orange Glaze.

1 1/3 cups milk

2 Tbsp Organic Culinary Lavender Buds

1/3 cup poppy seeds

4 cups all-purpose flour

2 Tbsp baking powder

1/3 cup granulated sugar

3/4 tsp salt

2 eggs, slightly beaten

1/4 cup honey

1/2 cup sunflower oil

1/2 cup fresh-squeezed orange juice

2 tsp fresh-grated orange zest (you'll need about 1 orange to make the zest—
see zesting tips on page 250)

Topping (optional)
Orange Glaze (see the recipe on the next page)

Preheat the oven to 350°F. Fill 2 muffin pans (12-cup size) with paper liners.

Combine the milk and lavender buds in a small saucepan. Bring the mixture to a boil over medium heat. Once the milk mixture begins to boil, remove from the heat, and stir. Allow the lavender buds to steep in the milk for 10 minutes. Strain the lavender buds from the milk, and discard the lavender buds. Add the poppy seeds to the milk, and let it stand for 20 minutes.

In a large mixing bowl, combine the flour, baking powder, sugar, and salt, and mix well. Make a well in the middle of the dry ingredients, and add the beaten eggs, honey, sunflower oil, orange juice, and orange zest, along with the lavender-infused milk. Lightly stir together just until the dry ingredients are moistened.

Fill each muffin cup 2/3 full with the batter. Bake at 350° for 20–25 minutes. Allow to cool, and drizzle with the optional Orange Glaze. Makes approximately 2 dozen muffins.

Orange Glaze

1 cup powdered
    (confectioners') sugar
3 Tbsp light cream
1 tsp orange extract

In a small bowl, mix together all the ingredients until smooth. Drizzle over Orange Lavender Poppy Seed Muffins.

Photo Courtesy of Jessica Criscenti

Recipe Tested in the Kitchen of Jessica Criscenti

Lavender Blueberry Muffins

From the moist cake brimming with plump blueberries to the bakery-style streusel topping, these Lavender Blueberry Muffins always win blue ribbons whenever I serve them. People aren't sure why they love my blueberry muffins so much, but I do—lavender and blueberries are an unbeatable pair!

1/3 cup granulated sugar

4 Tbsp butter, softened

1 egg, well-beaten

1 cup milk

1/2 tsp vanilla extract

2 1/3 cups all-purpose flour

4 tsp baking powder

1/2 tsp salt

1/2 tsp Organic Culinary Lavender Buds

1 1/2 cups blueberries, fresh OR frozen

Streusel Topping

1/2 cup granulated sugar

1 Tbsp packed brown sugar

1/3 cup all-purpose flour

1/2 tsp cinnamon

4 Tbsp butter, cut into chunks

Preheat the oven to 375°F. Well grease or paper line the cups of a 12-cup muffin tin.

In a mixing bowl, cream together the sugar and butter with an electric mixer for about 2 minutes, scraping down the sides of the bowl as needed. Add the egg, milk, and vanilla extract, and mix well. In a separate bowl, combine the flour, baking powder, salt, and lavender buds. Add the flour mixture, a little at a time, to the butter and egg mixture. Stir together until well incorporated. Fold in the blueberries. Spoon the batter into the prepared muffin pan, filling each cup 2/3 full.

Prepare the Streusel Topping by combining the sugars, flour, and cinnamon in a small bowl. Cut in the butter with a pastry blender or by hand until crumbly. Sprinkle some of the Streusel Topping over the muffins. Gently swirl the streusel into the top of the muffin, but be careful not to push the streusel too far down into the batter. Then top the muffins with the rest of the streusel. Bake at 375° for 25–30 minutes or until lightly brown. Makes 1 dozen muffins.

Photo Courtesy of Jessica Criscenti

Recipe Tested in the Kitchen of Jessica Criscenti

Lavender Apple Spice Muffins

Lavender's effect on this recipe is quite remarkable. You'll find yourself savoring every bite of these moist and delicious muffins, which taste very similar to an apple crisp!

1 tsp Organic Culinary Lavender Buds

2 cups all-purpose flour

1 cup oatmeal

2/3 cup granulated sugar

1 tsp salt

1 Tbsp plus 1 tsp baking powder

1 1/2 tsp ground cinnamon

1 1/2 tsp ground nutmeg

1/3 cup vegetable oil

1/3 cup applesauce

2 eggs, slightly beaten

1/3 cup milk

2 medium apples, peeled, cored, and diced

1/3 cup walnuts, finely chopped (optional)

Chef's Comments

For best results, use a crisp apple variety such as Gala or Jonathan.

Preheat the oven to 375°F. Fill 2 muffin pans (12-cup size) with paper liners. In a spice grinder or coffee grinder, chop the lavender buds until finely ground, or chop them up with a sharp knife. Set aside.

Mix together the flour, oatmeal, sugar, salt, baking powder, ground lavender buds, cinnamon, and nutmeg until well blended. Make a well in the center of the flour mixture, and add the oil, applesauce, eggs, and milk. Stir until all ingredients are well incorporated. Fold in the diced apples and walnuts, if desired, and mix well.

Fill the prepared muffin cups 2/3 full with the batter, and bake at 375° for 20–25 minutes or until a toothpick inserted in the center comes out clean. Cool the muffins on a wire rack. Makes approximately 1 1/2 dozen muffins.

Photo Courtesy of Debbie Walter

Recipe Tested in the Kitchen of Debbie Walter

Chocolate Chip Lavender Scones

These scones are absolutely amazing, and their aroma while baking is heavenly! The addition of buttermilk gives them a wonderful, light texture, and the chunks of chocolate are simply magnificent when paired with the lavender. Brushing the scones with an "egg wash" gives the tops a nice golden brown color, and the sugar adds a bit of crispness. When all combined—these Chocolate Chip Lavender Scones make an impressive presentation.

2 cups all-purpose flour

4 tsp granulated sugar

1/4 tsp salt

2 tsp baking powder

6 Tbsp unsalted butter, cut into pieces and allowed to soften

2 eggs, well-chilled

1/2 cup buttermilk, well-chilled

1 tsp vanilla extract

1 Tbsp Organic Culinary Lavender Buds

1/2 cup milk chocolate chips OR your favorite milk chocolate candy bar cut into chunks

Egg Wash

1 large egg, lightly beaten

1 Tbsp milk

Preheat the oven to 400°F, and lightly butter a cookie sheet. With a sifter or metal strainer, sift together the flour, sugar, salt, and baking powder in a large mixing bowl. Add the butter, and using a pastry blender, mix together until the butter and flour mixture form a coarse meal.

In a large measuring cup, beat together the eggs, buttermilk, and vanilla extract until well incorporated, and then pour over the dry ingredients. Stir just until the ingredients come together to form a soft dough. Do not over-mix. Gently fold in the lavender buds and chocolate chips, using care again not to over-mix the dough.

On a lightly floured surface, roll the dough out to a 3/4-inch thickness, and cut into triangles. Place the triangles on the prepared cookie sheet.

Make the egg wash by whisking together 1 lightly beaten egg with 1 Tbsp of milk. Brush the tops of the scones with this mixture, sprinkle with a little sugar, and immediately place them in the oven.

Bake the scones at 400° for 8–10 minutes or until they are nicely browned and an inserted toothpick in the center comes out clean. Makes approximately 16 scones.

Chef's Comments

For best results...

Make sure that all of the wet ingredients are cold.

When adding the liquid to the dry ingredients, do so all at once. Then mix everything together quickly and lightly.

Remember: A light hand makes a light scone.

Recipe Tested in the Kitchen of Evelyn Bradley

English Cream Scones with Lavender Lemon Curd

The trick to making perfect scones is all in the technique (see the "Chef's" box on page 217). These delightful treasures are the ideal accompaniment to a cup of tea, and when paired with my Lavender Lemon Curd, they become a delicacy fit for royalty!

2 cups all-purpose flour

4 tsp granulated sugar

1/4 tsp salt

2 tsp baking powder

6 Tbsp unsalted butter, cut into pieces and allowed to soften

1/2 cup heavy whipping cream

2 eggs, well-chilled

1 tsp vanilla extract

Lavender Lemon Curd (see the recipe on the next page)

Preheat the oven to 400°F. Lightly butter a cookie sheet. With a sifter or metal strainer, sift together the flour, sugar, salt, and baking powder in a large bowl. Add the butter, and using a pastry blender, mix together until the butter and flour mixture form a coarse meal. In a large measuring cup, stir together the cream, eggs, and vanilla extract, and then pour over the dry ingredients. Stir just until the ingredients come together to form a soft dough. Do not over-mix.

On a lightly floured surface, roll the dough out to a 3/4-inch thickness, and cut into triangles. Place the triangles on the prepared cookie sheet, and brush the top of the scones with a little cream. (This helps them to turn a nice golden brown during baking.) Bake the scones at 400° for 8–10 minutes or until they are nicely browned and an inserted toothpick in the center comes out clean. Serve with Lavender Lemon Curd. Makes approximately 16 scones.

Lavender Lemon Curd

6 Tbsp unsalted butter

3 Tbsp Organic Culinary Lavender
 Buds

1 cup fresh-squeezed lemon juice

2/3 cup granulated sugar

2 large eggs

2 egg yolks

2 tsp fresh-grated lemon zest (see
 zesting tips on page 250)

Photo Courtesy of Heidi Bitsoli

In a medium-size saucepan, melt the butter with the lavender buds, stirring gently, over a very low heat for 4 minutes. Remove the butter from the heat, and add the lemon juice. Allow the lavender buds to steep in the lemon juice and melted butter for an additional 4 minutes. Strain the lavender buds from the lemon butter, and discard the lavender buds. Return the lemon butter to the saucepan. Add the sugar, eggs, and egg yolks to the lavender-infused lemon butter. Using an electric mixer, beat the ingredients for about 2 minutes. The mixture will look curdled but will smooth out as it cooks. Cook over medium-low heat, whisking vigorously and continuously, until the lemon curd thickens, about 8–15 minutes. Do not let the mixture boil. The lemon curd is finished cooking when it is light yellow and coats the back of a spoon. Remove from the heat, and stir in the lemon zest. Transfer to a bowl, and cover by laying a piece of plastic wrap directly on top of the curd. Chill in the refrigerator for 2 hours before using. The curd will thicken more as it cools and can then be served with your favorite scones. When covered tightly, this curd may be stored in the refrigerator for up to 1 week or in the freezer for up to 1 month.

Recipe Tested in the Bitsoli Kitchen

Cranberry Almond Scones
with Lavender Devonshire Cream

Tea isn't merely a drink in England—it's a way of life. Scones, lemon curd, jam, and Devonshire cream are the ideal accompaniment for afternoon tea. My recipe for Lavender Devonshire Cream is thick but light, and its delicate sweet flavor flawlessly complements these lovely Cranberry Almond Scones.

2 cups all-purpose flour

4 tsp granulated sugar

1/4 tsp salt

2 tsp baking powder

6 Tbsp unsalted butter, cut into
    pieces and allowed to soften

2 eggs, beaten

1/2 cup heavy whipping cream

1 tsp orange extract

1/3 cup cranberries

1/3 cup sliced almonds

Lavender Devonshire Cream (see the
    recipe on the next page)

Preheat the oven to 400°F. Lightly butter a cookie sheet. With a sifter or metal strainer, sift together the flour, sugar, salt, and baking powder in a large bowl. Add the butter, and using a pastry blender, mix together until the butter and flour mixture form a coarse meal. In a large measuring cup, stir together the eggs, cream, and orange extract, and then pour over the dry ingredients. Add the cranberries and almonds. Stir just until the ingredients come together to form a soft dough. Do not over-mix.

On a lightly floured surface, roll the dough out to a 3/4-inch thickness, and cut into triangles. Place the triangles on the prepared cookie sheet, and brush the top of the scones with a little cream. (This helps them to turn a nice golden brown during baking.) Bake the scones at 400° for 8–10 minutes or until they are nicely browned and an inserted toothpick in the center comes out clean. Serve with Lavender Devonshire Cream. Makes approximately 16 scones.

Lavender Devonshire Cream

1 cup heavy whipping cream
2 Tbsp Organic Culinary Lavender Buds
1 container (4 oz. size) mascarpone cheese
3/4 tsp vanilla extract
1 1/2 Tbsp granulated sugar

In a medium-size saucepan, combine together the cream and lavender buds. Bring the mixture to a boil over medium heat. Once the cream begins to boil, immediately reduce the heat to low. Simmer for 10 minutes, stirring occasionally and using caution not to scald the cream. Remove from the heat, and strain the lavender buds from the cream. Discard the lavender buds, and place the lavender-infused cream in the refrigerator for at least 1 hour. Once the lavender-infused cream is completely cold, place it and the rest of the ingredients into a large bowl. Beat with an electric mixer until the mixture begins to thicken and is light and fluffy, about 8–12 minutes. Use immediately, or cover and refrigerate until ready to use.

Chef's Comments

The trick to making perfect scones is all in the technique (see the "Chef's" box on page 217).

Recipe Tested in the Kitchen of Sharon Bacis

Lavender Lane

Cakes, Pies & Tarts

Lavender Orange Chiffon Cake

*M*y mother often made orange chiffon cake, and it was always divine.
My version includes an infusion of lavender cream, which enhances
the flavor of the orange and gives her classic recipe even more appeal.
The secret to this cake's delicate texture is whipped egg whites—
the result is a lovely, light, and airy cake.

1 cup light cream

2 Tbsp Organic Culinary Lavender Buds

1 1/2 sticks unsalted butter, at room
  temperature

1 1/2 cups granulated sugar

1/4 cup orange juice

1 1/2 Tbsp fresh-grated orange zest, finely
  grated (see zesting tips on page 250)

1/2 tsp vanilla extract

2 1/3 cups self-rising cake flour

5 large egg whites, at room temperature

1/4 tsp cream of tartar

Photo Courtesy of Marcia Swiderski

Preheat the oven to 350°F. Butter and flour a Bundt pan. In a small saucepan,
stir together the cream and lavender buds. Cook over medium-high heat just
until the cream begins to bubble. Remove the pan from the heat, stir, and allow
the lavender buds to steep in the cream for 15 minutes. Strain the lavender
buds from the cream. Discard the lavender buds, and set the cream aside.

In a large mixing bowl, beat together the butter and sugar with an electric mixer on high speed until light and fluffy. Add the lavender-infused cream, orange juice, orange zest, and vanilla extract. Beat just until well blended. Reduce the mixer's speed to low, and gradually add the flour, scraping down the sides of the bowl as necessary. Again, beat just until well blended.

In a separate large bowl and using an electric mixer, beat the egg whites, with clean beaters, on medium speed until they become foamy. Add the cream of tartar, and increase the speed to medium-high. Continue to beat until the eggs form stiff peaks when the beaters are lifted, about 5 minutes.

Using a rubber spatula, gently fold 1/4 of the egg whites into the cake batter. Continue to gently fold the egg whites into the batter, 1/4 of them at a time, until all of the whites are mixed in. Be very gentle when folding in the egg whites, and use caution not to deflate the mixture. Pour the batter into the prepared Bundt pan.

Bake at 350° for 30–35 minutes. The cake is done when the top is slightly golden brown and it starts to pull away from the sides of the pan or when a wooden toothpick inserted in the center comes out clean. Cool for 15–20 minutes before removing from the pan. To remove, carefully turn the cake over. The cake should easily fall out of the pan. Place the cake on a serving plate, and allow it to cool for an additional 10 minutes.

Dust with powdered sugar, or frost with Lavender Vanilla Icing, which can be found on page 45. For even more orange taste, use the Orange Glaze found on page 211. Makes approximately 6–8 servings.

Recipe Tested in the Kitchen of Barbara Parr

Spiced Carrot Cake with Lavender Cream Cheese Frosting

Moist and delicious, this Spiced Carrot Cake has apples, raisins, and just a hint of orange peel. Its excellent taste seems too good to be true, especially when it's smothered with the Lavender Cream Cheese Frosting.

2 cups all-purpose flour

1 3/4 cups granulated sugar

1 tsp baking powder

1 tsp baking soda

1/2 tsp ground cinnamon

1/4 tsp ground cloves

1/4 tsp ground nutmeg

2 1/2 cups carrots, finely shredded

1/2 cup Granny Smith apples, finely shredded

1/2 cup golden raisins

1 cup sunflower oil

4 eggs

1/4 tsp vanilla extract

1 Tbsp fresh-grated orange zest (see zesting tips on page 250)

1/4 cup pecans, finely ground

Lavender Cream Cheese Frosting (see the recipe on the next page)

8 whole pecans and grated carrots (for garnish)

Preheat the oven to 350°F. Butter and lightly flour two 9-inch round baking pans or one 9-inch x 13-inch baking pan, and set aside.

In a large mixing bowl, combine together the flour, sugar, baking powder, baking soda, cinnamon, cloves, and nutmeg. Add the carrots, apples, raisins, oil, eggs, vanilla extract, and orange zest. Beat with an electric mixer on low speed for 1 minute. Increase the mixer's speed to medium, and continue to beat until all ingredients are well incorporated, about 3 minutes.

Fold in the ground pecans, and mix until well blended. Pour the batter into the prepared pan(s).

Bake at 350° for 30–35 minutes (round pans) or 35–40 minutes (9-inch x 13-inch pan) or until a toothpick inserted near the center comes out clean. Cool the cake for 10 minutes before removing from the pan(s).

Place the cake(s) on a serving plate(s), and cool thoroughly. Spread with Lavender Cream Cheese Frosting, and garnish with 8 whole pecans and grated carrots. Makes approximately 8 servings.

Lavender Cream Cheese Frosting

1/2 tsp Organic Culinary Lavender Buds

1 pkg (8 oz. size) low-fat cream cheese, at room temperature

1/2 cup butter, at room temperature

1 tsp vanilla extract

1 cup powdered (confectioners') sugar

In a spice grinder or a coffee grinder, chop the lavender buds until finely ground. In a large mixing bowl, beat together, using an electric mixer, the cream cheese, butter, and lavender buds for about 1 minute or until creamy. Add the vanilla extract, and mix until well blended. Scrape down the sides of the bowl with a spatula as needed. Slowly add the powdered sugar, a little at a time, continuing to scrape the sides of the bowl as necessary. Blend until the frosting is light and fluffy. Cover, and refrigerate until ready to use.

Recipe Tested in the Kitchen of Jan Wiley

Pineapple Lavender Dream Cake

This light, fresh, and fruity dessert is perfect for any celebration, and the layers of lavender cake, crushed pineapple, and vanilla pudding make it simply dreamy!

Cake
1 cup low-fat milk
2 Tbsp Organic Culinary Lavender
    Buds
1/4 cup plain nonfat yogurt
1/4 cup sunflower oil
1 tsp vanilla extract
1 egg yolk
1 cup granulated sugar, plus 1/2 cup,
    separated
4 egg whites, at room temperature
2 1/2 cups self-rising cake flour,
    sifted

Pineapple
1 can (9 oz. size) crushed pineapple

Topping
1/2 cup (4 oz.) light cream cheese
1/2 cup low-fat milk
1 pkg (3.4 oz. size) vanilla-flavored
    instant pudding
3/4 cup non-dairy whipped topping,
    plus 3/4 cup, separated (we prefer
    Cool Whip extra creamy)
1/2 cup walnuts, finely chopped

Spray the bottom of 1 round cake pan (10-inch size) with nonstick cooking spray. Do not coat the sides of the pan. Line the bottom with a 10-inch circle of waxed paper. Spray the waxed paper with additional cooking spray, and dust with flour. Set aside.

In a medium-size saucepan, combine together the milk and lavender buds. Bring the mixture to a boil over medium heat. Once the milk begins to boil, immediately reduce the heat to low. Simmer for 3–5 minutes, stirring occasionally and using caution not to scald the milk. Remove from the heat, and strain the lavender buds from the milk. Discard the lavender buds, and set aside the lavender-infused milk.

In a large mixing bowl, combine the yogurt, oil, vanilla extract, and egg yolk. With an electric mixer set on medium speed, beat until well blended. Add 1 cup of sugar, and beat well. Measure out 3/4 cup of the lavender-infused milk, and add it to the mixture, beating on medium-low speed until the sugar dissolves, about 2 minutes. Set aside the remaining lavender-infused milk (about 1 1/2 Tbsp).

In a separate bowl and using an electric mixer, beat the egg whites, with clean beaters, on high speed until they become foamy. Gradually add the remaining 1/2 cup of sugar, and continue to beat until stiff peaks begin to form, about 6 minutes. Gradually add the sifted cake flour to the yogurt mixture alternately with the egg white mixture, beating at a very low speed until all of the ingredients are well incorporated.

Preheat the oven to 375°F. Pour the batter into the prepared cake pan. Tap the pan on the counter to remove any air bubbles. Bake at 375° for 10 minutes. Reduce the oven temperature to 350°, and bake for an additional 24–28 minutes or until a wooden toothpick inserted in the center comes out clean. Remove from the oven, and allow the cake to cool for 10 minutes. Using a sharp knife, loosen the cake from the sides of the pan, and turn out onto a wire rack. Peel off the waxed paper, and let the cake cool completely.

Place the pineapple in a fine-mesh strainer to drain out the juice, and then press the fruit with a spatula to help drain the juice. Place the strainer over a bowl, and set aside, allowing any remaining juice to drain from the pineapple.

To make the Topping, in a medium-size bowl, beat the cream cheese with an electric mixer until creamy. Gradually beat in the milk for the topping, along with the reserved lavender-infused milk. Add the dry pudding mix, and continue to beat until well incorporated. Whisk in 3/4 cup of non-dairy whipped topping, and set aside the remaining 3/4 cup for later use.

Place the cake on a serving plate, and top evenly with the crushed pineapple. Top the layer of pineapple with the pudding mixture, spreading evenly. Spread the remaining 3/4 cup of non-dairy whipped topping over the layer of pudding, and garnish with the chopped walnuts. Chill for at least 2 hours before serving. Makes approximately 8 servings.

Recipe Tested in the Kitchen of Christina Schultz

Lemon Berry Torte with Lavender Buttercream

This dazzling dessert has layers of light lemony cake and tangy berry preserves. Best of all, it's topped with a distinguished buttercream frosting flavored with sweet lavender. This torte will make any occasion spectacular.

1 stick unsalted butter, at room temperature

1 Tbsp fresh-grated lemon zest, finely grated (see zesting tips on page 250)

1 1/2 cups granulated sugar

2 Tbsp vegetable oil

1/4 cup fresh-squeezed lemon juice

1/4 cup buttermilk, plus 1/2 cup, separated

2 1/4 cups self-rising cake flour

5 large egg whites

1/4 tsp cream of tartar

Lavender Buttercream (see the recipe on the next page)

1 cup raspberry preserves

Preheat the oven to 350°F. Butter and flour two 8-inch round cake pans. In a large mixing bowl, beat together the butter, lemon zest, and sugar with an electric mixer on high speed until light and fluffy. Add the vegetable oil, lemon juice, and 1/4 cup of buttermilk. Beat just until well blended. Reduce the mixer's speed to low, and gradually add the flour alternately with the remaining 1/2 cup of buttermilk, scraping down the sides of the bowl as necessary and beating just until well blended.

In a separate large bowl and using an electric mixer, beat the egg whites, with clean beaters, on medium speed until they become foamy. Add the cream of tartar, and increase the speed to medium-high. Continue to beat until the eggs form stiff peaks when the beaters are lifted, about 5 minutes.

Using a rubber spatula, gently fold 1/4 of the egg whites into the cake batter. Continue to gently fold the egg whites into the batter, 1/4 of them at a time, until all of the whites are mixed in. Be very gentle when folding in the egg whites, and use caution not to deflate the mixture.

Divide the batter evenly between the two prepared cake pans.

Bake at 350° for 35–40 minutes or until a wooden toothpick inserted in the center of the cakes comes out clean. Cool the pans on a wire rack for 15 minutes. Gently run a sharp knife against the sides of the pans to loosen the cake from the sides. Allow the cakes to cool for another 10 minutes, and then carefully turn the cakes over to remove them from the pans. Let the cakes cool completely on the rack, right side up.

Make the Lavender Buttercream, and set aside. Once the cakes are completely cool, cut them in half horizontally. To do so, hold the palm of one hand against the top of the cake, and using a long serrated knife, gently cut the cake in half horizontally. Repeat with the other cake. Place 1 layer of the cake on a serving plate, and spread 1/3 of the raspberry preserves over the top of it, leaving about a 1/4-inch border around the edge. Repeat these steps twice more, using 1/3 of the preserves each time, and top with the last layer of the cake. Frost the cake with the Lavender Buttercream. Makes approximately 8 servings.

Lavender Buttercream

3 Tbsp Half & Half OR light cream
2 Tbsp Organic Culinary Lavender Buds
2 cups powdered (confectioners') sugar
1/4 cup unsalted butter, softened
1/2 tsp vanilla extract

In a small saucepan, stir together the Half & Half and lavender buds. Cook over medium-high heat just until the Half & Half begins to bubble. Remove the pan from the heat, and allow the lavender buds to steep in the Half & Half for 15 minutes. Strain the lavender buds from the Half & Half. Discard the lavender buds, and chill the Half & Half in the refrigerator for 15 minutes or until cool. In a large bowl, beat together the sugar, butter, vanilla extract, and lavender-infused Half & Half until smooth and thoroughly mixed. If necessary, add a touch more of either Half & Half or powdered sugar until the frosting has a nice spreading consistency. Refrigerate until ready to use.

Recipe Tested in the Kitchen of Christina Schultz

Lavender Cheesecake

My Lavender Cheesecake is quite simple to prepare, but after one bite, people will think you spent hours creating this fabulous treat. It tastes outstanding when served with fresh berries and phenomenal when drizzled with warmed Chocolate Lavender Raspberry Jam, which can be found on page 304.

2 Tbsp butter, melted

6 Tbsp graham cracker crumbs

4 Tbsp almonds, finely ground

2 Tbsp heavy whipping cream

2 Tbsp Organic Culinary Lavender Buds

2 pkg (8 oz. size) cream cheese, at room temperature

2/3 cup granulated sugar, plus 3 Tbsp, separated

3 large eggs, slightly beaten

1/2 tsp vanilla extract, plus 1 tsp, separated

1 cup sour cream

Preheat the oven to 350°F. Combine together the melted butter, graham cracker crumbs, and ground almonds, and mix until well blended. Press the crust mixture into the bottom of a 9-inch springform pan. Set aside.

In a small saucepan, heat the heavy whipping cream and lavender buds over medium heat until the mixture begins to bubble. Remove from the heat, stir, and allow the lavender buds to infuse in the cream until after the cheesecake is removed from the oven.

In a medium-size mixing bowl, beat together the cream cheese, 2/3 cup of sugar, eggs, and 1/2 tsp of the vanilla extract with an electric mixer on medium speed. Continue to mix until all of the ingredients are smooth. Pour over the crust in the springform pan.

Bake at 350° for 25–30 minutes or until the cheesecake sets and appears dry on top. Turn the oven off. Remove the cheesecake from the oven, and set aside.

Strain the lavender buds from the cream with a fine-mesh strainer. Discard the lavender buds, and place the cream in a small mixing bowl. Add the remaining 3 Tbsp of sugar, sour cream, and remaining 1 tsp of vanilla. Mix until completely smooth, and spread the cream mixture over the warm cheesecake. Return the cheesecake to the oven, while still turned off, for 10 more minutes.

After the cheesecake has finished baking, allow it to cool to room temperature. Then cover, and refrigerate the cheesecake for at least 6 hours or overnight before serving. Before removing the cheesecake from the springform pan, run a sharp knife around the outside edge of the pan. Makes approximately 8 servings.

Photo Courtesy of Jessica Criscenti

Recipe Tested in the Kitchen of Jessica Criscenti

Lavender Peach Skillet Cobbler

*My Lavender Peach Skillet Cobbler boasts the same buttery flavor
and crunchy topping as old-fashioned cobblers, but it is made in a skillet!
This fruitful dessert offers a delightfully sweet ending to any meal.
It's best served warm and topped with ice cream, and I recommend using
Rich Lavender Honey Ice Cream, which can be found on page 290, for an
extra-decadent delight.*

Filling

3 cups fresh peaches, peeled, pitted, and sliced (frozen peaches may be used instead)

1 cup fresh blueberries OR raspberries (frozen berries may be used instead)

1/4 cup granulated sugar

1 tsp cornstarch

Topping

1 cup all-purpose flour

1 tsp baking powder

1/2 cup packed brown sugar

1/4 cup granulated sugar

1/4 tsp ground cinnamon

1/4 tsp ground nutmeg

1/2 tsp Organic Culinary Lavender Buds

5 Tbsp butter, very cold and cut into chunks

Preheat the oven to 425°F. In a large cast-iron skillet or ovenproof skillet, combine together the ingredients for the filling. Cook over medium heat until the mixture begins to bubble, about 2–3 minutes. Mix well, and remove from the heat.

In a medium-size mixing bowl, combine together the flour, baking powder, brown sugar, sugar, cinnamon, nutmeg, and lavender buds. With a pastry blender or with your hands, mix the butter in until the mixture is crumbly. Sprinkle over the fruit mixture. Place the cobbler in the oven, and bake, uncovered, at 425° for 30–40 minutes. Makes approximately 6–8 servings.

Photo Courtesy of Heidi Bitsoli

Recipe Tested in the Bitsoli Kitchen

French Lavender Four-Berry Pie

Nothing beats a summertime pie filled with locally grown fruits. Just imagine the aroma of apples, blackberries, raspberries, blueberries, strawberries, and rhubarb baking together in a buttery piecrust—and it tastes even better!

Crust

2 sticks unsalted butter

2 1/2 cups all-purpose flour, plus
    extra for rolling

1 tsp salt

2 Tbsp granulated sugar

1/2–1 cup ice water

Filling

1 cup granulated sugar

4 tsp quick-cooking tapioca

4 tsp ground cinnamon

1/2 tsp Organic Culinary Lavender
    Buds

1/2 cup fresh blackberries

1/2 cup fresh raspberries

1/2 cup fresh blueberries

1/2 cup strawberries, sliced

1 cup apples, peeled and sliced

1 cup fresh rhubarb, thinly sliced

2 Tbsp butter, cut up into small
    pieces

1 Tbsp granulated sugar (for garnish)

Cut the sticks of butter into 1/2-inch cubes, and place them in the freezer for 15 minutes. In a food processor, combine the flour, salt, and sugar. Pulse to mix well. Add the frozen butter cubes, and pulse until the mixture resembles a coarse meal. Add the water, 1 Tbsp at a time, pulsing until the mixture just begins to clump together. If you pinch some of the crumbly dough and it holds together, it's ready; if not, add a little more water, and pulse again. Remove the dough from the processor, and place it on a clean surface. Using care not to over-knead the dough, shape it into 2 round balls. Wrap the balls separately in plastic wrap, and refrigerate at least 1 hour.

Remove the crust balls from the refrigerator, and let them sit at room temperature for 5–10 minutes. On a well-floured surface, roll out one of the dough balls with a rolling pin to make a 12-inch circle (it will be about 1/8-inch-thick). While rolling, use a metal spatula to lift up the dough to check if it is sticking to the surface below. If necessary, add a few sprinkles of flour to keep the dough from sticking. Repeat with the other ball. Set one of the crusts aside, and gently fold the other pastry in half. Place the dough inside a 10-inch pie plate, lining up the fold with the center of the pan. Carefully unfold, and press the dough inside the pie plate. With a fork, prick the crust all over on the inside of the pie plate. This helps prevent air bubbles. Set aside.

Preheat the oven to 375°F. In a large mixing bowl, stir together the sugar, tapioca, cinnamon, and lavender buds. Add all of the fruits and the rhubarb, and toss gently until everything is well coated. Let stand for 15 minutes. Spoon the filling into the prepared pie plate, and dot with the pieces of butter. Trim the pastry even with the edge of the pie plate, and moisten the edge of the pastry with water. Place the remaining pastry sheet over the filling. Trim the top crust to 1/2 inch beyond the pie plate. Fold the top crust over the bottom edge, and crimp between your finger and thumb to create a decorative edge. Cut slits in the top pastry to allow the steam to escape. Place pieces of tin foil around the edge of the crust to protect it from over-baking.

Bake at 375° for 25 minutes. Remove the pie from the oven, remove the foil, and sprinkle with 1 Tbsp of sugar. Return the pie to the oven, and bake for an additional 20–25 minutes or until the crust is golden brown and the filling is bubbly. Cool on a wire rack. Makes approximately 6–8 servings.

Recipe Tested in the Kitchen of Bonnie Feldbush

Lemon Meringue Pie with Lavender Almond Butter Crust

My mother was an amazing cook and an even better baker. Her lemon meringue pie was always my favorite, and I often requested it for my birthday rather than a traditional cake. One of the things that made all of Mom's pies so memorable was the crust—it was buttery and flaky every time. For my Lemon Meringue Pie, I started with my mom's piecrust recipe and added ground almonds and lavender. This very unique crust, when it mingles with the lemon filling, creates a taste sensation that just has to be experienced!

Crust

1 stick unsalted butter

1/4 cup blanched almonds

1 Tbsp Organic Culinary Lavender Buds

1 cup all-purpose flour, plus extra for rolling

1/2 tsp salt

1/2 tsp packed brown sugar

2–3 Tbsp ice water

Filling

1 pkg Jell-O Lemon Cook & Serve Pudding & Pie Filling

3/4 cup granulated sugar

3 cups water

3 eggs

Meringue

3 egg whites

1/3 cup granulated sugar

Cut the stick of butter into 1/2-inch cubes, and place them in the freezer for 15 minutes. Grind the almonds in a spice grinder or coffee grinder until very fine. Add the lavender buds, and pulse together until well ground and blended. In a food processor, combine the flour, salt, and sugar, along with the ground almonds and lavender buds. Pulse to mix well. Add the frozen butter cubes, and pulse until the mixture resembles a coarse meal. Add the water, 1 Tbsp at a time, pulsing until the mixture just begins to clump together. If you pinch some of the crumbly dough and it holds together, it's ready; if not, add a little more water, and pulse again. Remove the dough from the processor, and place it on a clean surface. Using care not to over-knead the dough, shape it into a round ball. Wrap the ball in plastic wrap, and refrigerate at least 1 hour.

Remove the crust ball from the refrigerator, and let it sit at room temperature for 5–10 minutes. On a well-floured surface, roll out the dough with a rolling pin to make a 12-inch circle (about 1/8-inch-thick). While rolling, use a metal spatula to lift up the dough to check if it is sticking to the surface below. If necessary, add a few sprinkles of flour to keep the dough from sticking.

Preheat the oven to 350°F. Gently fold the circle in half, and place it inside a 10-inch pie plate, lining up the fold with the center of the pan. Carefully unfold, and press the dough inside the pie plate. With a fork, prick the crust all over on the inside of the pie plate. This helps prevent air bubbles. To make a decorative edge on the crust, either press the edge down with the tines of the fork or pinch the edge together with your fingers. Place tin foil around the edge of the crust to protect it from over-baking, but leave the bottom of the crust uncovered. Bake at 350° for 10–15 minutes or until the bottom is a light golden brown. Remove the piecrust from the oven, and set aside.

Using the ingredients listed under "Filling," prepare the lemon pie filling according to the "Traditional Pie Directions" on the side of the box. Fill the piecrust with the pudding, and set aside. To make the meringue, beat the egg whites in a large bowl using an electric mixer on high speed until they are foamy. Gradually add the sugar, and continue to beat until the eggs form stiff peaks. Spread over the filling, leaving the edge of the crust uncovered. Bake at 350° for 15–20 minutes or until the meringue turns a light golden brown. Cool at room temperature for at least 4 hours, and serve. Store any remaining pie in the refrigerator for up to 3 days. Makes approximately 6–8 servings.

Recipe Tested in the Kitchen of Arlene Hicks

Peanut Butter Banana Pie with Lavender Chocolate Drizzle

This pie is ideal for anyone who loves the combination of peanut butter and bananas. The smooth texture and low-fat content make this delicious dessert a big hit—and best of all, it's easy to prepare.

Pie

1 1/2 cups graham cracker crumbs

3 Tbsp butter, melted

1/3 cup low-fat cream cheese

1/3 cup peanut butter

1 pkg (3.4 oz. size) cheesecake-flavored OR vanilla-flavored pudding mix

1/4 cup packed brown sugar

1 1/2 cups milk

2 small bananas, sliced

1 cup non-dairy whipped topping

Lavender Chocolate Drizzle

3 Tbsp milk

1 Tbsp Organic Culinary Lavender Buds

1/2 cup semisweet chocolate chips

Place the graham cracker crumbs in a bowl with the melted butter, and mix until well incorporated. Press the mixture onto the bottom and up the sides of a 9-inch pie plate. Place the crust in the refrigerator while preparing the filling to allow the cracker crumbs to set.

In a large mixing bowl, beat the cream cheese and peanut butter with an electric mixer, set at medium-high speed, until smooth. Add the pudding mix and brown sugar. Continue to beat, scraping down the sides of the bowl as needed, until the ingredients are well blended. Reduce the speed to low, and add the milk, about 1/2 cup at a time. Continue to mix until the filling is smooth.

Place 1/3 of the pie filling into the prepared pie shell. Arrange the sliced bananas over the filling. Spoon the remaining 2/3 of the filling over the bananas, and spread evenly. Top with the whipped topping, cover, and refrigerate.

To make the Lavender Chocolate Drizzle, in a small saucepan, heat together the milk and lavender buds over medium heat until the milk begins to bubble. Reduce the heat to low, and simmer for 5 minutes, stirring occasionally and using caution not to scald the milk. Remove from the heat, and strain the lavender buds from the milk. Discard the lavender buds, and return the lavender-infused milk to the saucepan. Add the chocolate chips to the milk, and stir over low heat until the chocolate melts.

Allow the chocolate to cool to room temperature, and then drizzle it over the pie. Cover, and refrigerate the pie for at least 4–6 hours before serving. Makes approximately 6–8 servings.

Photo Courtesy of Debbie Walter

Recipe Tested in the Kitchen of Debbie Walter

Lavender Key Lime Parfaits

My Lavender Key Lime Parfaits are a fun alteration of the traditional Key lime pie, which can make the tongue and taste buds leap with glee. This parfait version dances with pizzazz and the glorious flavors of lavender and real Key limes. With each spoonful, you'll feel as if you were vacationing in the Florida Keys!

1 can (14 oz. size) fat-free sweetened
  condensed milk

1 Tbsp Organic Culinary Lavender Buds

2 Tbsp granulated sugar

1/2 cup fresh-squeezed lime juice
  (preferably from Key limes)

1/2 tsp fresh-grated lime zest (see
  zesting tips on page 250)

1 egg

2 egg yolks

1 1/2 cups graham cracker crumbs

1 container (8 oz. size) Cool Whip non-dairy whipped topping

grated lime rind or finely chopped walnuts (for garnish)

Chef's Comments

If you are unable to find Key limes, regular limes may be used instead. The flavor of these parfaits will be slightly different when using regular limes—but it will still be delicious!

In a medium-size saucepan, combine the milk and lavender buds. Bring the mixture to a boil over medium heat. Once the milk begins to boil, immediately reduce the heat to low, and simmer for 15 minutes, stirring occasionally and using caution not to scald the milk. Remove from the heat, and strain the lavender buds from the milk. Discard the lavender buds, and return the lavender-infused milk to the saucepan.

In a medium-size mixing bowl and using a handheld wire whisk, beat together the sugar, lime juice, lime zest, egg, and egg yolks until smooth. Pour the mixture into the saucepan with the lavender-infused milk, and heat over medium-high heat, stirring constantly with the whisk, until the mixture begins to bubble. Reduce the heat, and simmer for about 6 minutes, stirring constantly. Remove from the heat. Place the saucepan in a large ice-filled bowl for about 15 minutes or until the mixture reaches room temperature. While the mixture is cooling, stir occasionally with the whisk.

To create the parfaits, set out 8 (8 oz. size) glasses. Spoon 1 Tbsp of the graham cracker crumbs into each glass. Then add 3 Tbsp of the lime mixture to each. Top with 1 Tbsp Cool Whip. Repeat the layers once, ending with the Cool Whip. Top the parfaits with a dollop of the lime mixture, and garnish with grated lime rind or finely chopped walnuts. Serve immediately. Makes 8 servings.

Photo Courtesy of Heidi Bitsoli

Recipe Tested in the Bitsoli Kitchen

Fascinating Facts

Key limes versus regular limes—what's the difference? Key limes are much smaller and rounder than regular limes and tend to be quite seedy. They also have a very distinct, aromatic flavor.

Luscious Strawberry & Lavender Cream Tart

This recipe reminds me of a dreamy summer afternoon, and it always ends up being a big hit. It looks stunning, the flavors come together effortlessly, and the classic combination of strawberries and cream tastes simply superb on top of the light and delicious pastry dough.

Pastry Dough

1/4 cup (2 oz.) cream cheese, softened
1 stick butter, softened
1 1/4 cups all-purpose flour

Spray a 9 1/2-inch or 10-inch tart shell with nonstick cooking spray.

To make the pastry dough, blend together the cream cheese and butter with a spatula or wooden spoon until completely smooth. Add the flour, and continue to mix until smooth. Don't over-work the dough, or it will be hard after you bake it. On a lightly floured surface, roll the dough into a circle that will fit into the tart pan. Place the rolled-out pastry dough into the center of the tart shell, and gently flatten it into the pan, working your way up the sides to the rim. Place the tart shell in the refrigerator

for at least 45 minutes to allow the dough to chill.

Preheat the oven to 350°F. Remove the tart shell from the refrigerator, and prick the dough several times with a fork all over the bottom to allow the steam to escape as it bakes. Cut a round piece of aluminum foil or parchment paper large enough to fit inside the tart pan and halfway up the sides. Place the foil or parchment over the dough, and then pour dry beans or place pie weights on top to prevent the crust from puffing up as it bakes.

Bake at 350° for 8 minutes or until the edges of the tart are a light golden brown. Remove the foil/parchment and beans/weights, and bake the tart for an additional 5 minutes or just until the bottom of the dough begins to brown. Remove the tart shell from the oven, and cool completely before filling.

Lavender Cream and Strawberries

1/2 cup light whipping cream
2 Tbsp Organic Culinary Lavender Buds
1/2 cup white chocolate chips
6 Tbsp unsalted butter
1/2 cup granulated sugar
2 Tbsp sour cream
1/2 tsp vanilla extract
2 eggs
1 pound fresh strawberries, stemmed, washed, and sliced
melted white chocolate (for garnish—optional)

In a small saucepan, stir together the cream and lavender buds. Cook over low heat just until the cream begins to bubble. Remove the pan from the heat, stir, and allow the lavender buds to steep in the cream for 15 minutes. Strain the lavender buds from the cream. Discard the lavender buds. Return the lavender-infused cream to the saucepan.

Stir in the white chocolate chips. Over low heat, continue to stir until the chocolate is completely melted.

Remove from the heat, and allow the mixture to cool to room temperature.

In a medium bowl, beat together the butter and sugar with an electric mixer on high speed until smooth, about 8–10 minutes. Add the chocolate mixture, and continue to mix until well incorporated, scraping down the sides of the bowl as necessary. Add the sour cream, vanilla extract, and eggs, and beat until well blended.

Spoon the Lavender Cream into the prepared pastry shell. Cover the sides of the tart crust with aluminum foil, and bake at 350° for an additional 15 minutes. Remove from the oven, and cool on a wire rack. Once the tart is completely cooled, arrange the strawberry slices evenly over the cream, and drizzle with melted white chocolate, if desired. Refrigerate the tart for at least 1 hour before serving. Makes approximately 6–8 servings.

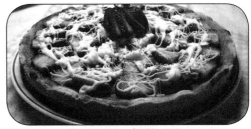

Photo Courtesy of Debbie Walter

Recipe Tested in the Kitchen of Debbie Walter

Lavender Pecan Pie Tartlets

These miniature pies are lovely to enjoy with an afternoon tea or as a sweet ending to a light lunch.

Crust

1/4 cup (2 oz.) cream cheese, softened

1 stick butter, softened

1 1/4 cups all-purpose flour

1 tsp Organic Culinary Lavender Buds

Filling

3/4 cup packed light brown sugar

1 Tbsp butter

1 egg

1 tsp vanilla extract

1 1/4 cups pecans, chopped

To create the crust, blend together the cream cheese and the stick of butter until completely smooth. Add the flour, and continue to mix until well blended.

Grind the lavender buds in an electric spice grinder or coffee grinder, and then add them to the dough, mixing until well incorporated. Refrigerate the dough for 2 hours.

You will need enough mini-muffin pans to give you 24 mini-muffin cups. Spray the cups with nonstick cooking spray.

Roll the chilled dough into 24 balls. Place one pastry ball into each of the muffin cups. Press the dough to cover the bottom and sides of each cup.

Preheat the oven to 350°F.

For the filling, in a medium-size mixing bowl, combine the brown sugar, 1 Tbsp butter, egg, vanilla extract, and chopped pecans. Beat with an electric mixer until all ingredients are well blended.

Place the filling into the center of each pastry crust, about 1/2 full. Bake the pecan tarts at 350° for 20–25 minutes.

After they are cool, you can store the tartlets in an airtight tin at room temperature for up to 1 week or in the freezer for up to 1 month. Makes 2 dozen tartlets.

Recipe Tested in the Kitchen of Leah Dzierzawski

Lavender Lane

Cookies
& Sweets

Lavender Lemon Shortbread Cookies

This version of my lavender shortbread has turned into a Lavender Festival favorite. Every year, festival customers request to purchase these by the dozen. Not just your average cookie, this shortbread contains lemon and lavender, which really enhance its rich buttery texture.

1 1/2 cups unsalted butter, softened

1 cup granulated sugar

1 1/2 tsp vanilla extract

2 tsp fresh-squeezed lemon juice

2 tsp fresh-grated lemon zest (you'll need
    about 2 large lemons to make the zest)

1 1/2 Tbsp Organic Culinary Lavender
    Buds

1/4 tsp salt

3 cups all-purpose flour

coarsely ground sugar (for garnish)

In a medium-size mixing bowl, cream together the butter, sugar, vanilla extract, lemon juice, lemon zest, lavender buds, and salt with an electric mixer for about 4–5 minutes or until the mixture is light and fluffy. Continuing to use the electric mixer, slowly add the flour, one cup at

Chef's Comments

When zesting citrus fruits…

It's easier to use fruits that are stored at room temperature.

———

Use a zester or the fine holes on a grater.

———

Rub the fruit across the grater until the color comes off in small crumbs.

———

Do not grate the pith (the white part), or the zest will taste bitter.

a time, until well incorporated. If the dough is still sticky, add a touch more flour. Form the dough into 2 logs, each about 2–3 inches in diameter. Wrap the logs in plastic wrap, and refrigerate them until firm, about 1 hour.

Preheat the oven to 325°F. Slice the dough into 1/2-inch-thick slices. Lay the cookie slices on a parchment-lined baking sheet. Sprinkle the top of each cookie with coarsely ground sugar, if desired. Bake at 325° for 10–15 minutes or until the edges are slightly golden. Allow the cookies to cool completely on wire racks before serving. Makes approximately 3 dozen cookies.

Photo Courtesy of Julie Kampling

Variation

To create a traditional-looking shortbread cookie, make the dough according to the recipe, but do not form the logs. Instead, lightly spray a cookie sheet with nonstick cooking spray, and then press the dough into the cookie sheet, covering the whole sheet. The dough should be about 1/2-inch-thick. Prick the dough all over with a fork to prevent bubbles. The prick marks can be in decorative patterns, but make sure they are at least 1 1/2–2 inches apart. Bake in a 325°F oven for 15–20 minutes or until the sides are golden brown. Remove from the oven, and cool for 5 minutes. Using a pizza cutter, immediately cut the shortbread into 2-inch squares. Remove from the pan, and enjoy!

Recipe Tested in the Kitchen of Julie Kampling

Italian Sesame Cookies with Lavender Vanilla Icing

This authentic Italian recipe has been passed down from generation to generation in my husband's family, and his Aunt Pat, who is a fabulous baker, recently shared it with us. These toasty and crunchy sesame seed cookies are flavorful but not too sweet; plus, they're great for breakfast or with a cup of coffee. And we just couldn't resist adding our favorite ingredient: lavender, which gives them a unique burst of flavor.

4 cups all-purpose flour

1 cup granulated sugar

1 Tbsp baking powder

1/4 tsp salt

1 cup shortening

2 eggs, slightly beaten

1/2 cup milk

1 tsp vanilla extract

1 1/2 cups sesame seeds

Lavender Vanilla Icing (see the recipe on the next page)

Preheat the oven to 375°F. In a large mixing bowl, combine the flour, sugar, baking powder, and salt. Mix until well incorporated. Add the shortening, and mix with a pastry blender or by hand until the mixture resembles a coarse meal. Add the eggs, milk, and vanilla extract. Blend well.

Take small amounts of dough, about 1 Tbsp, and shape into little loaves. Roll each cookie loaf in sesame seeds until well coated (there may be sesame seeds left over after you are done). Place the loaves on a well-greased cookie sheet, and bake at 375° for 15–20 minutes or until a light golden brown. Remove from the cookie sheet, and allow to cool. When the cookies are cool, drizzle with Lavender Vanilla Icing. Makes approximately 4 dozen cookies.

Lavender Vanilla Icing

6 Tbsp milk

3 tsp lavender buds

2 Tbsp butter, softened

1/8 tsp salt

1/4 tsp vanilla extract

2 cups powdered (confectioners') sugar

In a microwave-safe bowl, add the milk and lavender buds, and heat in the microwave for 20 seconds on high power. Allow the lavender buds to steep in the milk for 15 minutes. Strain the lavender buds from the milk, and discard the lavender buds. Return the lavender-infused milk to the bowl. Add the remaining ingredients to the milk, and beat with an electric mixer until smooth. If necessary, add a touch more of either milk or powdered sugar until the icing is the consistency that you prefer.

Photo Courtesy of Mary Marlatt

Recipe Tested in the Kitchen of Mary Marlatt

Lavender Almond Crescents

Afternoon tea and almond crescents—a match made in heaven. This recipe adds a touch of lavender to this buttery cookie, turning a classic into an absolute delight. One of my favorite rainy-day reprieves includes a cup of Earl Grey, a good book, and a couple of these fabulous cookies.

2 sticks butter, at room temperature

1/3 cup powdered (confectioners') sugar, plus more for dusting

1/3 cup granulated sugar

1/2 tsp almond extract

1/4 tsp vanilla extract

1 cup blanched almonds, finely chopped

2 tsp Organic Culinary Lavender Buds

2 1/2 cups all-purpose flour

Preheat the oven to 350°F. Spray a cookie sheet with nonstick cooking spray.

With an electric mixer, cream together the butter, powdered sugar, and granulated sugar, scraping down the sides of the bowl as needed, until light and fluffy. Add the almond extract and vanilla extract, and mix until smooth.

Mix in the almonds and lavender buds until well incorporated. Add the flour, a little at a time, and mix thoroughly.

Take 2 Tbsp of the dough, and roll it into a ball, about 1 inch in diameter.

Then roll the ball lengthwise into a cylinder, and form it into a crescent shape. Repeat until all the dough is used. Place the cookies on the prepared cookie sheet, and bake at 350° for 15–20 minutes or until a light golden brown.

Cool the cookies completely, and then dust with powdered sugar. Makes approximately 3 dozen cookies.

Variation

After the cookies have cooled, dip one end in melted chocolate, and then sprinkle with chopped almonds instead of the powdered sugar.

Photo Courtesy of Katrina Godbout

Recipe Tested in the Kitchen of Katrina Godbout

Spanish Wedding Cookies with Lavender Powdered Sugar

This recipe is my version of the classic Spanish Wedding Cookie (or snowball cookie). I've added malted milk powder, which gives these treats unparalleled taste; plus, the Brazil nuts add a delectable crunch. Spanish Wedding Cookies are everyone's favorite and always disappear rather quickly.

2 sticks unsalted butter, softened

1/4 cup granulated sugar

1/4 cup powdered (confectioners') sugar

1/4 tsp sea salt

1 tsp vanilla extract

1/2 cup malted milk powder

1 cup all-purpose flour

1 cup malt flour

1 cup Brazil nuts OR pecans, chopped very fine

Lavender Powdered Sugar

1 tsp Organic Culinary Lavender Buds

1/3 cup powdered (confectioners') sugar

Chef's Comments

If you cannot find malt flour, you can use all-purpose flour instead.

Preheat the oven to 375°F.

Using an electric mixer, blend together the butter, granulated sugar, 1/4 cup powdered sugar, salt, and vanilla extract for 3–4 minutes or until the ingredients are creamy and fluffy.

Stir in the malted milk powder and the flours, one cup at a time, just until blended. Mix in the chopped nuts.

Roll the dough into 1-inch balls. Place the balls 1 inch apart on a nonstick baking sheet. Bake at 375° for 15–20 minutes or until the cookies are lightly browned around edges. Remove from the cookie sheet, and cool on a wire rack.

To make the Lavender Powdered Sugar, grind together the lavender buds and the 1/3 cup powdered sugar in a food processor or blender, with the lid firmly attached, until the ingredients are well blended.

Place the Lavender Powdered Sugar in a large Ziploc-type bag. Roll the cooled cookies in the powdered sugar, thoroughly coating each one. Place them on a cookie plate, or store in a container. Makes approximately 4 dozen cookies.

Recipe Tested in the Kitchen of Mary Marlatt

Lavender Sour Cream Twists

These cookies were a staple in my home while I was growing up, and it was usually a battle to see which of the five siblings would get the "last one." I modified my mother's recipe a bit so that they are rolled in a Lavender Vanilla Sugar rather than just plain sugar. The lavender and vanilla add a wondrous taste to these already remarkable cookies.

Sour Cream Twists

1/4 cup warm milk

1 pkg (1/4 oz. size) quick active dry yeast

3 1/2 cups flour

1 tsp salt

1/2 cup butter

1/2 cup margarine

1 cup sour cream

1 egg, plus 2 egg yolks

1/2 tsp vanilla extract

Lavender Vanilla Sugar

1 vanilla bean OR 1/2 tsp vanilla extract

2 cups granulated sugar

1 Tbsp Organic Culinary Lavender Buds

Chef's Comments

We highly recommend using a jelly roll pan or a cookie sheet with a rim when baking these cookies to prevent the melting sugar from possibly dripping onto the bottom of the oven. Flat baking sheets are not recommended for this recipe.

Photo Courtesy of Julie Kampling

Heat the milk over medium heat until it begins to bubble. Remove from the heat, and stir in the yeast. Set aside, and allow the yeast to dissolve. In a large mixing bowl, sift together the flour and salt. With a pastry blender or by hand, cut the butter and margarine into the flour until it resembles a coarse meal. Add the milk and yeast, sour cream, eggs, and vanilla extract. Mix thoroughly, cover with a damp cloth, and refrigerate for at least 2 hours or overnight.

To prepare the Lavender Vanilla Sugar, cut the vanilla bean lengthwise, and scoop out the seeds from the inside with a butter knife or the edge of a spoon. Set the seeds aside, and discard the bean. Place the sugar, lavender buds, and vanilla seeds in a food processor, and pulse 10–12 times or until the ingredients are well blended.

Place 1/2 cup of the Lavender Vanilla Sugar on a clean surface, and spread it into a 6-inch diameter circle. Remove the dough from the refrigerator, and divide in half. Place half of the dough (it will be very sticky) in the center of the sugar, and turn it over once to coat both sides with the sugar. Roll the dough with a pastry roller or rolling pin into an 8-inch x 11-inch rectangle. Fold the dough in half, sprinkle with about 3 Tbsp of the Lavender Vanilla Sugar, and roll into an 8-inch x 11-inch rectangle again. Repeat the steps for rolling twice more, using about 3 Tbsp of the sugar each time.

Preheat the oven to 375°F. Roll the dough to about a 1/4-inch thickness, and cut into strips about 1 inch wide x 4 inches long. Twist the ends in opposite directions, stretch, and place them on an ungreased cookie sheet, pressing down the ends to hold the twist in place. Bake at 375° for 15 minutes or until they are light golden brown. Immediately, remove the cookies from the sheet, and cool on a wire rack. Store in a covered container for up to 1 week. Makes approximately 2 dozen cookies.

Repeat with the other half of the dough, or if you prefer, it can be wrapped tightly, and stored in the freezer for later use for up to 1 month. To use, thaw the dough in the refrigerator for 24 hours before rolling in the sugar and baking.

Recipe Tested in the Kitchen of Julie Kampling

Lavender Pistachio Biscotti

These tasty cookies are baked twice, which gives them their famous crunchy texture and appeal. The flavors of lavender, orange, and pistachio blend together beautifully, making these biscotti the ideal accompaniment to your favorite cup of coffee or hot chocolate.

2 1/4 cups all-purpose flour

1 tsp baking powder

1/2 tsp baking soda

1/4 tsp salt

2/3 cup granulated sugar

3 large eggs

3 Tbsp raw honey

1/2 tsp vanilla extract

2 Tbsp fresh-grated orange zest (see zesting tips on page 250)

2 Tbsp Organic Culinary Lavender Buds, crushed

1/2 cup pistachios, chopped

Preheat the oven to 350°F. Sift together the flour, baking powder, baking soda, and salt. Set aside.

In a large bowl, whip the sugar and eggs until the mixture turns a light lemony color. Stir in the honey, vanilla extract, orange zest, and lavender buds. Gently fold in the dry ingredients to form a dough-like mixture. Add the pistachios, and mix in.

Divide the dough into 6 equal portions. Using a little flour, shape each section into a 7-inch-long by 1-inch-high log. Place the logs on a parchment paper-lined baking sheet, and place in the oven.

Bake at 350° for 20–25 minutes or until the dough pops back up when lightly pressed with a finger. Remove from the oven, and cool for 10 minutes on a wire rack.

Reduce the oven temperature to 275°F.

Using a serrated knife, slice each log into 4 slices, 1/2-inch-thick. Lay the slices on the baking sheet, and place in the 275° oven until firm, about 15 minutes.

Remove from the oven. When completely cool, store the biscotti in an airtight container. Makes approximately 24 biscotti.

Recipe Tested in the Kitchen of Linda Mascagni

Blueberry Lavender Foldovers

These sophisticated cookies are a breeze to make and truly a gourmet's delight. The lavender and blueberry centers awaken the senses and tantalize the taste buds. The original recipe is from my husband's Aunt Pat, who makes them with raspberry preserves. My family has tried other fruit centers, but we always come back to lavender and blueberry—those two flavors commingle so well.

1/2 cup unsalted butter, cut into chunks

3 oz. cream cheese, cut into chunks

1 1/2 cups all-purpose flour

1/2 tsp salt

1 Tbsp milk

1/4 cup ice water

1/2 cup blueberry preserves

1 tsp Organic Culinary Lavender Buds

powdered (confectioners') sugar (for dusting—optional)

Preheat the oven to 400°F.

Place the butter and cream cheese into a food processor. Add the flour and salt, and pulse several times, scraping down the sides of the bowl with a spatula every so often. Add the milk and water through the feed tube while the machine is on. The dough should not be smooth, but rather like popcorn in appearance.

Once the ingredients are well incorporated, divide the dough in half, and form into 2 balls. On a well-floured surface, roll out each half of the cookie dough to 1/8-inch thickness. Cut each half into about 10 squares; each square should be about 2 inches wide.

In a small bowl, mix together the blueberry preserves and lavender buds. Blend well.

Place 1/2 tsp of the preserves in the center of each square. Dampen the sides of the pastry square with water, and fold over, creating a triangle. Pinch the edges together firmly.

Place the pastries on a well-greased cookie sheet, and bake at 400° for 10–12 minutes or until lightly browned. Immediately remove the cookies from the sheet, and place them on a cooling rack. After the pastries are completely cooled, dust them with powdered sugar, if desired. Makes approximately 20 cookies.

Chef's Comments

A food processor cuts the preparation time for these pastries in half, but they are still just as wonderful if mixed by hand. If you prefer to hand-mix, simply use a handheld pastry blender, and follow the steps.

Recipe Tested in the Kitchen of Mary Marlatt

Lavender Gingersnaps

These molasses cookies are flavored with fresh-ground ginger and organic lavender, turning Grandma's artful recipe into an absolute masterpiece. Enjoy them with coffee or tea, or for an extra-decadent dessert, serve these Lavender Gingersnaps with my recipe for Rich Lavender Honey Ice Cream, which can be found on page 290.

3/4 cup butter, softened

1/2 cup packed brown sugar

1/2 cup granulated sugar

1 egg, slightly beaten

2 Tbsp orange juice

1/4 cup organic blackstrap molasses

2 1/4 cups all-purpose flour

2 tsp baking soda

1/2 tsp salt

2 Tbsp fresh gingerroot, finely minced

1/2 tsp ground cinnamon

1/2 tsp ground cloves

Photo Courtesy of Heidi Bitsoli

Lavender Sugar Topping

3/4 cup turbinado sugar (coarsely ground sugar may be used instead)

1 Tbsp Organic Culinary Lavender Buds

In a large mixing bowl, cream together the butter and the brown and granulated sugars with an electric mixer until light and fluffy. Add the egg, orange juice, and molasses, and continue to beat until well incorporated. In a separate bowl, combine the flour, baking soda, salt, gingerroot, and spices, and mix well. Slowly add the dry ingredients to the butter mixture, and continue to mix until well blended. Chill the dough for 1 hour.

In the meantime, combine the turbinado sugar and lavender buds in a spice grinder or coffee grinder, and blend until the lavender buds are ground a bit and blended well with the sugar. Place this Lavender Sugar Topping on a plate, and set aside.

Preheat the oven to 350°F. Line a cookie sheet with parchment paper, or well grease the cookie sheet instead. Remove the chilled dough from the refrigerator, and roll the dough into 1-inch balls. When all the balls are formed, roll them in the Lavender Sugar Topping. Place the sugared balls on the prepared cookie sheet, about 3 inches apart. Bake at 350° for 8–10 minutes or until the cookie tops puff up, crack, and then deflate in the oven. Cool the cookies on a wire rack, and store them in an airtight container for up to 1 week. Makes approximately 4 dozen cookies.

Chef's Comments

We prefer using fresh gingerroot in these cookies. In our opinion, it gives them the best taste. However, if you don't have fresh gingerroot on hand, a 1/2 tsp of dried ground ginger may be used instead.

For chewier cookies, remove them from the oven when the tops have puffed up and cracked— and when most of them have begun to deflate. For crunchier cookies, bake an additional minute until the edges are a golden brown.

Recipe Tested in the Bitsoli Kitchen

Tiramisu Trifle with Lavender Mocha Cream

If you've never had the pleasure of tasting tiramisu, you are in for a real treat. From the sweetened mascarpone filling with cocoa and lavender to the shavings of chocolate nestled between layers of espresso-infused cake, every bite of my Tiramisu Trifle with Lavender Mocha Cream will bring joy to your taste buds. This classic Italian dessert seems complex, but it is quite simple to make. It does require a few extra steps, but the end result is nothing short of superb!

1 1/2 cups light whipping cream

1 Tbsp Organic Culinary Lavender Buds

1 pkg (10 oz. size) Sara Lee free & light pound cake, cut into 1-inch cubes (you can use regular pound cake instead, if you prefer)

1 cup espresso OR strongly brewed coffee, cold

2 containers (8 oz. size) mascarpone cheese

1/3 cup, plus 1 Tbsp powdered (confectioners') sugar

2 tsp unsweetened cocoa powder (we prefer Hershey's special dark)

1 tsp vanilla extract

1/4 cup milk chocolate chips, finely chopped

1/4 cup bittersweet chocolate chips, finely chopped

2 cups non-dairy whipped topping (we prefer Cool Whip extra creamy)

chocolate curls (for garnish—optional)

a mint sprig and fresh raspberries (for garnish—optional)

In a medium-size saucepan, stir together the cream and lavender buds. Cook over medium heat just until the cream begins to bubble. Remove the pan from the heat, stir, and allow the lavender buds to steep in the cream for 20 minutes. Strain the lavender buds from the cream.

Discard the lavender buds. Chill the cream in the refrigerator for at least 4 hours or overnight before using. (The cream and coffee are best when prepared the night before.)

Cover the bottom of a glass trifle dish with half of the pound cake. Drizzle half of the coffee over the pound cake. Set aside.

In a medium-size bowl and using an electric mixer set on medium-high, beat together the mascarpone cheese, powdered sugar, cocoa powder, and vanilla extract, along with the lavender-infused whipping cream, until smooth. Continue mixing on medium-high speed until the mixture forms stiff peaks.

Spoon half of the cheese mixture over the pound cake, spreading it evenly. Sprinkle half of the milk chocolate chips and bittersweet chocolate chips over the cheese mixture. Top with half of the whipped topping.

Repeat all of the layers in the same order, ending with the whipped topping on top. Cover, and chill for at least 6 hours before serving. Garnish with chocolate curls or a mint sprig and fresh raspberries, if desired. Makes approximately 12 servings.

Chef's Comments

For the best flavor, we suggest using an Italian espresso, such as Lavazza, which can be found at most Italian markets or gourmet food stores.

Fascinating Facts

Originally from Lombardy, Italy, mascarpone cheese is a rich, buttery Italian cream cheese. Soft in texture and delicate in flavor, mascarpone is created from the cream in cow's milk. It is rumored that the milking cows used for mascarpone cheese are fed a special diet of grasses, herbs, and flowers, which produces a fresh-tasting milk—but only the cows know for sure if the rumor is true.

Recipe Tested in the Kitchen of Alene Soloway

Lavender Profiteroles with Chocolate Mousse & Cinnamon Cream

"Profiterole" comes from an Old French word meaning "profit" or "small gift." More commonly known as "cream puffs," these pastries are made from a classic French recipe for "pate a choux," which I infused with the sweet scent of lavender. When served with Chocolate Mousse and Cinnamon Cream, these light pastries certainly offer a luxurious taste of the good life.

1 1/3 cups water
1 stick butter, plus 1 tsp, cubed
1 Tbsp Organic Culinary Lavender
    Buds
1 1/4 cups all-purpose flour
4 large eggs
Chocolate Mousse (see the recipe on
    the next page)
Cinnamon Cream (see the recipe on
    the next page)

Preheat the oven to 350°F. In a large saucepan, combine together the water, butter, and lavender buds. Bring the mixture to a boil, and then reduce the heat. Simmer for 4 minutes. Remove from the heat, and strain the lavender buds from the water and butter. Return the water and butter mixture to the saucepan.

Gradually sift in the flour, about 1/4 cup at a time, while beating with a wooden spoon. Stir well until smooth, eliminating the white spots of flour. Place the pan over very low heat, and continue to beat the mixture until it is solid enough to leave the sides of the pan clean.

Remove from the heat, and allow the paste to cool to just above room temperature. Mix in the eggs, one by one, beating thoroughly each time. Although the paste may seem as if it will not mix with the eggs, be persistent. As you continue to beat the eggs into the paste it becomes easier to work with. In the end, the paste should be shiny and fairly soft but firm enough to hold its shape when dropped from a spoon.

Lightly butter a baking sheet, or use a nonstick pan. Scoop up spoonfuls of the dough with two teaspoons, and drop onto the baking sheet about 3–4 inches apart. Bake at 350° for 35–40 minutes or until the pastries are firm, well puffed, and brown. As soon as the pastries are removed from the oven, pierce them with a sharp knife to allow the steam to escape—if you don't do this, they will collapse. Transfer the pastries to a wire rack, and allow them to cool. Once cooled, stuff the pastries with the Chocolate Mousse, and top with the Cinnamon Cream just before serving. Makes approximately 18 profiteroles.

Chocolate Mousse

1 pkg (8 oz. size) low-fat cream cheese
1/2 cup cocoa powder
1 cup powdered (confectioners') sugar
1 1/2 tsp vanilla extract
2 cups light whipping cream

In a large bowl, combine together the cream cheese and cocoa. Beat well until smooth and fluffy. Add the powdered sugar and vanilla, and beat until smooth. In a separate medium-size bowl, beat the cream with an electric mixer until stiff peaks form. Fold the cream into the chocolate mixture. Cover, and refrigerate until ready to use.

Cinnamon Cream

1 cup heavy whipping cream
1 Tbsp granulated sugar
1 tsp cinnamon

In a medium-size mixing bowl, whip the cream with an electric mixer until it holds stiff peaks. Sprinkle with the sugar and cinnamon, and whip for 2 more minutes. Cover, and refrigerate until ready to use.

Recipe Tested in the Kitchen of Alene Soloway

Candied Lavender Citrus Slices

I absolutely love the tang of citrus fruits and find these candied citrus peels to be deliciously fresh—especially when they are kissed with the flavor of lavender. Orange, lemon, lime, or grapefruit peels can all be candied to make this zesty treat.

3 lemons

3 oranges (we prefer using clementines)

2 cups cold water, plus 2 cups, separated

3 Tbsp Organic Culinary Lavender Buds

3 cups granulated sugar, plus 1 cup, separated

Line a baking sheet with parchment paper, and set aside. Thoroughly wash the lemons and oranges, and pat them dry. Cut the fruits into quarters, and carefully peel the rind away from the fruit, keeping the peels intact as much as possible. Set the fruit from the lemons and oranges aside, reserving them for another use.

Using a sharp knife, cut the pith (the bitter white part of the citrus rind) away from the underside of the peels. The remaining peel should be approximately 1/8-inch-thick. It is fine if small amounts of the white pith remain. Slice the peels into long, thin strips, about 1/2-inch-wide.

Place the citrus peels in a large saucepan, and add 2 cups of cold water and the lavender buds. Bring the mixture to a boil over medium-high heat. Once the water begins to boil, reduce the heat to medium-low, and simmer for about 10 minutes without stirring. Drain the peels, and discard the water and lavender buds. It is fine if a few of the lavender buds still remain on the peels.

Return the citrus peels to the saucepan, and evenly sprinkle them with 3 cups of sugar. Add the remaining 2 cups of cold water to the sugared slices, and simmer over medium-high heat for about 15 minutes. The syrup will barely cover the tops of the peels, but do not stir during this process because it will cause the sugar to clump.

Remove the saucepan from the heat, and allow it to cool. Once cool, drain the peels in a colander. Preheat the oven to 250°F. Place the remaining 1 cup of sugar in a small bowl. Roll the peels in the sugar until they are well coated, and place them on the prepared baking sheet. Add more sugar if necessary.

Bake the sugar-coated peels at 250° for 30 minutes. Remove them from the oven, turn the slices over, and place them on a drying rack for at least 2 hours before serving. Once the peels are completely dry, scrape off any large sugar clumps, if necessary. Store the peels in an airtight container for up to 1 week. Makes approximately 1 pound.

Chef's Comments

For an extra-decadent treat, dip the Candied Lavender Citrus Slices in melted chocolate before serving.

—◈◈◈—

These colorful candied peels also make a beautiful edible garnish for cakes, cookies, and desserts.

Recipe Tested in the Kitchen of Sharon Bacis

Sesame & Lavender Honey Candies

These chewy candies are made with lavender-infused honey, which gives them a pronounced hint of herbaceous goodness. These healthful treats offer a great boost of energy and can even help cure a sweet tooth—naturally.

1/2 cup Organic Culinary Lavender Buds, ground
1 1/2 cups pure honey
2 1/2 cups sesame seeds

In a spice grinder or coffee grinder, chop the lavender buds until they are moderately ground and the oils are released from the buds.

In a heavy saucepan, stir together the ground lavender and the honey, and cook over medium heat until the mixture begins to bubble. Immediately remove from the heat, and allow the lavender buds to infuse in the honey for at least 1 hour, stirring often.

Heat the honey again over medium heat until it has a thin consistency. With a metal strainer, remove all of the lavender buds from the honey. Discard the lavender buds. Wipe the saucepan clean, removing any remaining lavender buds, and return the strained honey to the pan.

Add the sesame seeds to the honey, and gently cook over medium-high heat, stirring often, for about 10–12 minutes or until the mixture is golden brown.

(The candy is ready when a drop of the honey, placed in cold water, forms a soft ball.)

Pour the honey mixture onto a baking sheet lined with parchment paper. Using a buttered spatula, spread the candy over the pan. Allow it to cool to room temperature. After the candy has cooled, place it in the refrigerator, and chill for an additional 2–3 hours.

Remove the candy from the refrigerator, and allow it to reach room temperature once again. Peel off the parchment paper. With kitchen shears or a sharp knife, cut the candy into small rectangles, about 3 inches long by 1 inch wide. Wrap the candies individually in waxed paper, and store in a tin box. Makes approximately 2 dozen candies.

Chef's Comments

Sesame seeds can be quite expensive when purchased at the local supermarket, which most commonly sells them prepackaged in small amounts. For the most economical purchase, look for stores that sell sesame seeds in bulk, such as a bulk food store or health food store—that way, you can buy exactly the amount you need.

Photo Courtesy of Julie Kampling

Recipe Tested in the Kitchen of Julie Kampling

Lavender Lane

Smoothies, Ice Cream & Sorbet

Strawberry Lavender Orange Smoothie

This smoothie is simple to make, and any berries can be substituted for the strawberries. My family has used raspberries with fantastic results, but we're still partial to the strawberries.

1 1/2 cups low-fat milk

2 tsp Organic Culinary Lavender Buds

1 pint strawberries, stemmed, washed, and sliced

2/3 cup low-fat vanilla yogurt

3 Tbsp frozen orange juice concentrate

3 Tbsp raw honey

6 ice cubes

fresh orange slice or a strawberry (for garnish)

In a small saucepan, heat the milk over medium heat just until it begins to bubble. Remove from the heat, and add the lavender buds. Allow to steep for 4 minutes. Strain the lavender buds from the milk, and discard the lavender buds. Chill the lavender-infused milk for 10 minutes.

In the meantime, combine the remaining ingredients in a blender or food processor, and blend until smooth. Add the lavender-infused milk, and blend until well mixed. Garnish with a fresh orange slice or a strawberry. Makes approximately 4 servings (1 cup size).

Photo Courtesy of Heidi Bitsoli

Recipe Tested in the Bitsoli Kitchen

Berry Lavender Smoothie

Everyone loves milk shakes, but I strive to create more healthful alternatives for my family. This low-fat recipe combines delicious berries, honey, and a hint of flaxseed (although you would never know it); plus, it contains antioxidants, vitamin C, and loads of fruity flavor.

1 cup low-fat milk

2 tsp Organic Culinary Lavender Buds

1 1/2 cups frozen mixed berries, slightly thawed (strawberries, blueberries, blackberries, and raspberries all work wonderfully)

1 banana, chilled and peeled

1/4 cup low-fat plain yogurt

2 Tbsp fresh-squeezed orange juice

1 Tbsp flaxseed oil

1 Tbsp raw honey

a fresh mint sprig or berries (for garnish)

In a small saucepan, heat the milk over medium heat just until it begins to bubble. Remove from the heat, and add the lavender buds. Allow to steep for 4 minutes. Strain the lavender buds from the milk, and discard the lavender buds. Chill the lavender-infused milk for 10 minutes. In the meantime, combine the remaining ingredients in a blender or food processor, and blend until smooth. Add the lavender-infused milk, and blend until well mixed. Garnish with a fresh mint sprig, berries, or both. Makes approximately 2 servings.

Variation

For even more health benefits, add 1 Tbsp wheat germ and 1 Tbsp protein powder for a powerhouse of goodness!

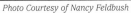
Photo Courtesy of Nancy Feldbush

Recipe Tested in the Kitchen of Linda Mascagni

Tropical Smoothie with Lavender & Lime

This ever-so-easy smoothie is from a good friend of mine who loves having fresh fruit in the morning. Four flavor sensations—floral lavender, sweet banana and pineapple, aromatic mango, and tart lime—combine to produce a wonderful tropical treat for the taste buds. Plus, the mango's dense fruit flesh creates such a creamy beverage that nothing else is needed to make this smoothie thick and luscious.

1/2 cup water

1/2 tsp Organic Culinary Lavender Buds

1 banana, peeled and broken in half

1 cup fresh pineapple, peeled, cored, and cut into pieces

1 mango, peeled and cut into chunks (discard the large pit)

juice from 1/2 lime (about 1 1/2–2 Tbsp)

4 ice cubes

Place all the ingredients in a blender in the order listed. Blend on a high speed for a few minutes or until all the ingredients are smooth. Makes approximately 2 servings.

Photo Courtesy of Debbie Walter

Recipe Tested in the Kitchen of Debbie Walter

Strawberry Lavender Kiwi Ice Cream

Store-bought ice cream pales next to this scrumptious treat. From the first spoonful to the last, the sweet, fruity flavor of this frozen delicacy proves that nothing compares to homemade ice cream.

1/4 cup granulated sugar, plus 3/4 cup, separated

1 tsp Organic Culinary Lavender Buds

2 ripe kiwis (kiwifruits), peeled

6 ripe strawberries, stemmed, washed, and sliced

1 tsp vanilla extract

3 Tbsp fresh-squeezed lemon juice

1 cup whole milk

2 cups heavy whipping cream

kiwi or strawberry slices or a sprig of lavender (for garnish)

Freeze the insert of an ice cream maker according to the manufacturer's instructions. In a spice grinder or electric coffee grinder, add the 1/4 cup of sugar and the lavender buds. Pulse 15–20 times or until the lavender buds are finely ground in the sugar. Set aside this "lavender sugar" for later use.

Puree the kiwis in a food processor. Place the kiwi in a bowl, and sprinkle with half of the lavender sugar. In a separate bowl, combine the strawberries, vanilla extract, lemon juice, and the other half of the lavender sugar. Stir gently. Cover and refrigerate both of the fruit mixtures for 1 1/2–2 hours.

In a mixing bowl, combine the milk and the 3/4 cup of sugar. Using an electric mixer, beat the milk mixture on low speed until the sugar is completely dissolved, about 2 minutes. Add the cream, kiwi puree, and any accumulated juice from the strawberries. (Do not add the strawberry slices at this time, just the juice.) Stir until smooth.

Turn the ice cream maker to the ON position, and slowly pour the milk and kiwi mixture into the maker through the ingredient spout. Let the ingredients mix until thickened, about 25–30 minutes. Add the sliced strawberries during the last 5 minutes of freezing.

Photo Courtesy of Valerie Harms

Transfer the ice cream to an airtight container, and place in the freezer for at least 1 hour before serving. If the ice cream becomes frozen solid, allow it to thaw at room temperature for a 1/2 hour before serving. Serve with a fresh slice of kiwi or strawberry, a sprig of lavender, or all three. Makes approximately 6–8 servings.

Recipe Tested in the Kitchen of Valerie Harms

Mocha Ice Cream with Lavender Chocolate-Covered Cherries

Your family and friends will marvel over this luscious yet so-easy-to-make ice cream. The mocha, lavender, and cherry flavors create a taste sensation that can only be described as wonderful.

Ice Cream

2 cups chocolate low-fat milk, well-chilled

3/4 cup granulated sugar

1 tsp instant espresso powder

1 cup heavy whipping cream, well-chilled

Chocolate-Covered Cherries

1/2 cup bittersweet chocolate chips

3/4 tsp Organic Culinary Lavender Buds

1/3 cup fresh Bing cherries, halved, pitted, and cut into pieces (canned cherries may be used, but drain the syrup before using)

> ## Chef's Comments
>
> *Instant espresso powder can be purchased at most gourmet food markets. If you cannot find instant espresso, you may use instant coffee instead.*

Freeze the insert of an ice cream maker according to the manufacturer's instructions.

With an electric mixer, whisk together the chocolate milk, sugar, and espresso powder for 2 minutes or until the sugar and espresso are completely dissolved. Add the cream, and stir until well blended. Turn the ice cream maker to the ON position, and slowly pour the milk mixture into the freezer bowl through the ingredient spout. Let the ingredients mix until thickened, about 30 minutes.

To make the chocolate-covered cherries, combine the chocolate chips and lavender buds in a microwave-safe bowl. Melt in the microwave (at 50% power) in 30-second increments, stirring each time until the chocolate is completely smooth. Add the cherries, and mix well. Spread the chocolate-covered cherries on a cookie sheet lined with parchment paper, and place in the freezer to harden, about 15 minutes. Remove from the freezer, and break into small pieces.

Photo Courtesy of Valerie Harms

During the last 5 minutes of mixing, add the chocolate-covered cherry pieces to the ice cream maker. Transfer the ice cream to an airtight container, and put in the freezer to harden. Makes approximately 6–8 servings.

Recipe Tested in the Kitchen of Valerie Harms

Toasted-Coconut Lavender Ice Cream

My family loves coconut ice cream after a meal at our favorite Thai restaurant—and we savor every spoonful. Determined to make it at home, I started with my basic ice cream recipe and added a touch of toasted coconut and lavender. The result was this heavenly treat. Try serving it with a slice of fresh pineapple or mango for a delightful taste of the tropics.

2 cups Half & Half

2 tsp Organic Culinary Lavender Buds

1/2 cup sweetened flake coconut

1 cup sweetened condensed milk

1/2 cup Egg Beaters OR egg substitute

1 can (15 oz. size) coconut cream

1/2 tsp rum extract

a slice of fresh pineapple or mango (for garnish)

Freeze the insert of an ice cream maker according to the manufacturer's instructions.

In a medium-size saucepan, combine the Half & Half and lavender buds. Bring to a boil over medium heat. Once the Half & Half begins to boil, immediately reduce the heat to low. Simmer for 3–5 minutes, stirring occasionally and using caution not to scald the milk. Remove from the heat, and strain the lavender buds from the Half & Half. Discard the lavender buds. Set aside the lavender-infused Half & Half to cool completely.

In the meantime, preheat the oven to 350°F. On a cookie sheet, spread the coconut in a single layer, and bake for 10–15 minutes or until light golden brown. Turn and check the coconut frequently to prevent burning. Remove from the oven, and allow to cool completely. Set aside.

With an electric mixer, whisk together the condensed milk, egg substitute, coconut cream, and rum extract, along with the lavender-infused Half & Half, for 1–2 minutes or until well blended. Place the ingredients in the refrigerator, and chill for 2 hours.

Turn the ice cream maker to the ON position, and slowly pour the mixture into the freezer bowl through the ingredient spout. Let the ingredients mix until thickened, about 30 minutes.

During the last 5 minutes of mixing, add the toasted coconut to the ice cream maker. Transfer the ice cream to an airtight container, and put in the freezer to harden. Makes approximately 6–8 servings.

Recipe Tested in the Kitchen of Linda Mascagni

Lavender Tiramisu Ice Cream

My frozen version of the classic tiramisu is rich and satisfying and can be prepared in about half an hour. Mascarpone cheese can be found at most supermarkets, and it adds a smooth and creamy texture to this delectable ice cream. Serve in espresso or cappuccino cups, add a lady finger to each, and top with shaved chocolate for an appealing touch.

Ice Cream

3 1/4 cups fat-free Half & Half (we prefer Land O'Lakes brand)

2 Tbsp Organic Culinary Lavender Buds

3/4 cup granulated sugar

1 tsp Dutch-process cocoa powder

1 Tbsp instant espresso powder

1/2 tsp coffee liqueur (you can substitute vanilla extract for the coffee liqueur, if you prefer)

ladyfingers and shaved dark chocolate (for garnish—optional)

Filling

1 container (8 oz. size) mascarpone cheese

1/2 tsp vanilla extract

1/4 cup granulated sugar

1/4 cup fat-free Half & Half

1 bar (4 oz. size) Ghirardelli 60% cacao bittersweet baking bar, finely chopped

Chef's Comments

Mascarpone cheese is a bit pricey but well worth the money since it makes the filling in this dessert richer than you can imagine.

Freeze the insert of an ice cream maker according to the manufacturer's instructions. In a small saucepan, combine 1/2 cup of the Half & Half and the lavender buds. Bring the mixture to a boil over medium heat. As soon as it begins to bubble, remove from the heat. Allow the lavender buds to steep in the Half & Half for 10 minutes. Strain the lavender buds from the Half & Half, and discard the lavender buds.

With an electric mixer, whisk together the lavender-infused Half & Half, along with the remaining Half & Half, sugar, cocoa powder, espresso powder, and coffee liqueur for 2 minutes or until the sugar and espresso are completely dissolved. Stir until well incorporated. Turn the ice cream maker to the ON position, and slowly pour the mixture into the freezer bowl through the ingredient spout. Let the ingredients mix until thickened, about 30 minutes. Make the filling by combining the mascarpone cheese, vanilla extract, sugar, and Half & Half. Blend well with an electric mixer until smooth and creamy. Fold in the chocolate, and mix well. Place the filling in a large plastic freezer bag, and set aside.

When the ice cream is finished thickening, spoon 1/3 of it into a freezer-safe container. Take the filling-packed plastic freezer bag, and cut off a 1-inch section of one of the corners. Swirl half of the filling over the ice cream. Spoon another 1/3 of the ice cream into the container, and then swirl the remaining filling over that layer. Finish spooning the remaining ice cream on top of that. With a butter knife, lightly swirl together the filling and ice cream in a zigzag pattern. Place the ice cream in the freezer to harden for about 4 hours before serving. Garnish with a ladyfinger and shaved dark chocolate, if desired. Makes approximately 6–8 servings.

Photo Courtesy of Jennifer Vasich

Recipe Tested in the Kitchen of Linda Mascagni

Rich Lavender Honey Ice Cream

My husband, who is an ice cream fanatic, says the flavor of this frozen dessert is utterly amazing and unlike anything he has ever tried! With the addition of the eggs and cream, the recipe actually makes a frozen custard (also called French ice cream), which is much richer and creamier than ordinary ice cream. Bon appétit!

1 cup whole milk, plus 1 Tbsp

2 cups heavy whipping cream

2 Tbsp Organic Culinary Lavender Buds

2 Tbsp raw honey

2 large eggs

3 large egg yolks

3/4 cup granulated sugar

1 tsp vanilla extract

Freeze the insert of an ice cream maker according to the manufacturer's instructions.

In a medium-size saucepan, combine together the milk, cream, and lavender buds. Bring the mixture to a boil over medium heat. Once the cream mixture begins to boil, immediately reduce the heat to low. Simmer for 3–4 minutes, stirring occasionally and using caution not to scald the milk. Remove from the heat, and strain the lavender buds from the cream mixture. Discard the lavender buds. Add the honey to the cream mixture, and stir until completely smooth. Set aside. In a mixing bowl, combine the eggs, egg yolks, sugar, and vanilla extract. Using an electric mixer, beat the egg combination on medium speed for about 2 minutes until the mixture is pale orange with a thick, smooth texture.

Reduce the mixer's speed to low, and slowly add the cream mixture to the eggs, adding about 1 cup at a time. When thoroughly combined, pour the egg and cream mixture back into the saucepan. Cook, stirring constantly, over medium heat until the mixture is thick enough to coat the back of the spoon (do not boil). Transfer the custard mixture to a bowl, and cover with a sheet of plastic wrap placed directly on the custard. Chill, covered, until cold, at least 3 hours or overnight.

Photo Courtesy of Maureen Buecking

Freeze the custard in an ice cream maker, and let it mix until thickened, about 25–35 minutes. Transfer the ice cream to an airtight container, and put in the freezer to harden. Makes approximately 6–8 servings.

Recipe Tested in the Kitchen of Maureen Buecking

Chocolate Lavender Custard

This custard is simply the best. The chocolate and lavender mingle together fabulously, creating an ultra-rich and decadent dessert. A little goes a long way—by serving this frozen dessert in a decorative teacup with a demitasse spoon, you can save on calories while indulging in a bit of elegance.

2 1/4 cups Half & Half

2 Tbsp Organic Culinary Lavender Buds

1/2 cup bittersweet chocolate chips

2 large eggs

1 cup granulated sugar

1 tsp vanilla extract

1/8 tsp salt

Freeze the insert of an ice cream maker according to the manufacturer's instructions. In a medium-size saucepan, combine the Half & Half and lavender buds. Bring to a boil over medium heat. Once the Half & Half begins to boil, immediately reduce the heat to low. Simmer for 3–5 minutes, stirring occasionally and using caution not to scald the milk. Remove from the heat, and strain the lavender buds from the Half & Half. Discard the lavender buds. Add the chocolate chips to the Half & Half, and stir until completely smooth and melted. Set aside.

In a separate mixing bowl, whisk the eggs with an electric mixer for about 1–2 minutes until they are light and fluffy. Add the sugar, vanilla extract, and salt. Beat on medium speed for about 2 minutes until the mixture is pale yellow with a thick, smooth texture. Reduce the mixer's speed to low, and slowly add the chocolate mixture to the eggs, a little at a time. Beat continuously until all ingredients are well mixed.

When thoroughly combined, pour the mixture back into the saucepan. Cook, stirring constantly, over medium heat until the mixture is thick enough to coat the back of the spoon (do not boil). Transfer the custard mixture to a bowl, and cover with a sheet of plastic wrap placed directly on the custard. Chill, covered, until cold, at least 3 hours or overnight.

Freeze the custard in an ice cream maker, and let it mix until thickened, about 25–35 minutes. Transfer the custard to an airtight container, and put in the freezer to harden. Makes approximately 4 servings.

Variation

To make Rocky Road Ice Cream, add 1/4 cup chocolate chips, 1/3 cup mini-marshmallows, and 1/4 cup chopped almonds to the custard during the last 5 minutes of mixing.

To transform this recipe into a German Chocolate Sundae, simply scoop the Chocolate Lavender Custard into sundae cups, add chopped pecans and toasted coconut, and drizzle your favorite chocolate dessert topping over it all.

Photo Courtesy of Jennifer Vasich

Recipe Tested in the Kitchen of Maureen Buecking

Lavender Watermelon Sorbet

This sorbet is one of the most refreshing ways to keep cool in the summer. Although there are a lot of seedless watermelons on the market today, I prefer to use the old-fashioned ones. The seeds are super easy to remove, and I am convinced that the non-genetically altered varieties taste much better.

3 cups water

1 cup granulated sugar

2 tsp Organic Culinary Lavender Buds

8 cups watermelon, cubed with the seeds and rind discarded

1/4 cup fresh-squeezed lime juice

1/8 tsp sea salt

a sprig of fresh mint (for garnish)

Freeze the insert of an ice cream maker according to the manufacturer's instructions.

To begin, you will need to make a "lavender simple syrup." In a medium-size saucepan, combine the water and sugar, and bring to a boil over medium-high heat. Reduce the heat to low, and simmer, stirring gently, about 3–5 minutes or until the sugar is completely dissolved. Remove from the heat, stir in the lavender buds, and allow them to steep for 3 minutes. Strain the lavender buds from the water, and discard the lavender buds. Completely cool the lavender simple syrup in the refrigerator for 4 hours or overnight.

The lavender simple syrup can be made in larger quantities to keep on hand for making other sorbets. To do so, simply double or triple the syrup part of the recipe, and keep it refrigerated. When you're ready to make your frozen dessert, use 3 cups of the syrup. For best results, use the syrup within 2 weeks.

To make the sorbet, add the watermelon, lime juice, and salt to a food processor. Puree for 1–2 minutes or until smooth. Combine the cooled lavender simple syrup and watermelon puree. Stir, and chill for 2 hours or overnight.

Turn the ice cream maker to the ON position, and slowly pour the watermelon mixture into the freezer bowl through the ingredient spout. Let the ingredients mix until thickened, about 25–30 minutes. Transfer the sorbet to an airtight container, and put in the freezer for 2 hours before serving.

If the sorbet becomes frozen solid, allow it to thaw at room temperature for 15–20 minutes before serving. Serve with a sprig of fresh mint, or try the nifty serving suggestion in the "Variation" box. Makes approximately 8 servings.

Variation

Melt 1 cup white chocolate chips in a microwave or double boiler. Add a few drops of green food coloring, and stir. When the chocolate is slightly cooled, pour it into the cups of a muffin pan. Roll the chocolate around the cups to cover the sides a bit, about 1 inch high. Freeze the chocolate cups until hard. Then pop them out, and use them as serving cups for the Lavender Watermelon Sorbet. Add a few chocolate chips to the top, and your guests will be delighted at the sweet watermelonesque presentation!

Recipe Tested in the Kitchen of Maureen Buecking

Raspberry Lavender Sorbet

Sorbet is a frozen delicacy made with sweetened fruit puree. It is naturally low in fat because it does not contain animal products. Sorbet can be a dessert or served between courses to cleanse the palate. Raspberry is perhaps the most popular flavor, and when combined with lavender, it makes the taste buds sing. This recipe calls for frozen berries, but fresh berries can be used too.

3 cups water

1 cup granulated sugar

2 tsp Organic Culinary Lavender Buds

3 cups frozen red raspberries, slightly thawed

1/2 cup frozen strawberries, slightly thawed

1/3 cup fresh-squeezed lime juice

1/4 cup light corn syrup

a whole raspberry or a sprig of lavender (for garnish)

Freeze the insert of an ice cream maker according to the manufacturer's instructions. To begin, you will need to make a "lavender simple syrup." In a medium-size saucepan, combine the water and sugar, and bring to a boil over medium-high heat. Reduce the heat to low, and simmer, stirring gently, about 3–5 minutes or until the sugar is completely dissolved. Remove from the heat, stir in the lavender buds, and allow them to steep for 3 minutes. Strain the lavender buds from the water, and discard the lavender buds. Completely cool the lavender simple syrup in the refrigerator for 4 hours or overnight.

The lavender simple syrup can be made in larger quantities to keep on hand for making other sorbets. To do so, simply double or triple the syrup part of the recipe, and keep it refrigerated. When you're ready to make your frozen dessert, use 3 cups of the syrup. For best results, use the syrup within 2 weeks.

Variation

Any combination of berries can be used in this recipe. Simply omit the raspberries and strawberries, and replace with 3 1/2 cups of your favorite combination of frozen berries, such as blackberries, blueberries, or boysenberries.

To make the sorbet, combine the raspberries, strawberries, and lime juice in a food processor, and blend for about 1–2 minutes or until the berries are completely pureed. Press the berries through a fine-mesh strainer to remove all the seeds. Combine the raspberry puree with the cooled lavender simple syrup and the corn syrup. Stir, and chill for 2 hours or overnight.

Turn the ice cream maker to the ON position, and slowly pour the raspberry mixture into the freezer bowl through the ingredient spout. Let the ingredients mix until thickened, about 25–30 minutes. Transfer the sorbet to an airtight container, and put in the freezer for 2 hours before serving. Serve with a whole raspberry, a sprig of lavender, or both. Makes approximately 8 servings.

Photo Courtesy of Maureen Buecking

Recipe Tested in the Kitchen of Maureen Buecking

Lavender Lemon Italian Ice

Sweetened, flavored ice. It's simple, it's natural, and it's believed to be the oldest frozen dessert on record. Story after story is told about ancient people enjoying snow saturated with honey and fruit. Much more advanced than fruit-flavored snow, this modern recipe blends together the tartness of fresh lemons and the sweet essence of lavender. The result is a light, refreshing, and oh-so-delicious medley that is sure to make its own history.

4 cups water

1 cup granulated sugar

2 Tbsp Organic Culinary Lavender Buds

1 1/2 cups fresh-squeezed lemon juice (about 4 medium lemons) (use only fresh-squeezed; do not use bottled lemon juice)

1 tsp fresh-grated lemon zest (see zesting tips on page 250)

a fresh slice of lemon or a sprig of lavender (for garnish)

Freeze the insert of an ice cream maker according to the manufacturer's instructions.

To begin, you will need to make a "lavender simple syrup." In a medium-size saucepan, combine the water, sugar, and lavender buds. Bring the mixture to a boil over medium-high heat, stirring continually until the sugar is completely dissolved. As soon as the mixture begins to boil, immediately remove it from the heat, and allow the lavender buds to steep in the syrup for 3–5 minutes. Strain the lavender buds from the water, and discard the lavender buds. Completely cool the lavender simple syrup in the refrigerator for 4 hours or overnight.

Chef's Comments

To get the most juice out of citrus fruits, allow them to first reach room temperature. Next, firmly roll them over the counter or other hard surface with the palm of your hand prior to juicing. This will not only help improve juice yields but also make it easier to extract the juice, especially if you are squeezing the fruits by hand.

Variation

For a spectacular treat, make this Lavender Grapefruit Italian Ice…

Substitute 1 1/2 cups fresh-squeezed pink grapefruit juice and 1 tsp finely grated grapefruit zest for the lemon ingredients. Also add 2 Tbsp orange juice concentrate to the mixture, and follow the rest of the steps.

The lavender simple syrup can be made in larger quantities to keep on hand for making other Italian ices. To do so, simply double or triple the syrup part of the recipe, and keep it refrigerated. When you're ready to make your frozen dessert, use 4 cups of the syrup. For best results, use the syrup within 2 weeks.

To make the Italian ice, combine the cooled lavender syrup, lemon juice, and lemon zest. Stir well.

Turn the ice cream maker to the ON position, and slowly pour the lemon and lavender mixture into the freezer bowl through the ingredient spout. Let the ingredients mix until thickened, about 25–30 minutes.

Transfer the Italian ice to an airtight container, and put in the freezer to harden. Serve with a fresh slice of lemon, a sprig of lavender, or both. Makes approximately 8 servings.

Recipe Tested in the Kitchen of Jan Wiley

Lavender Lane

Lavender
& Chocolate

Vanilla Lavender Hot Chocolate

It was the ancient Maya and Aztecs of Mesoamerica who first enjoyed drinking chocolate, but their drinks were bitter or spicy. Rich, creamy drinks like this one didn't exist until chocolate made its way to Europe—and sugar was finally added. This recipe creates an intriguing flavor that no powdered mix could ever compete with. Smooth and velvety, but not too sweet, this is how hot chocolate was meant to be made.

2 cups Half & Half

1 1/2 Tbsp Organic Culinary Lavender Buds

3/4 cup dark chocolate chips OR semisweet chocolate chips OR 60% cacao
    bittersweet chocolate chips (we prefer Ghirardelli chips)

1 1/2 tsp vanilla extract

fresh whipped cream and shaved chocolate (for garnish)

In a medium-size saucepan, combine the Half & Half with the lavender buds. Cook over medium-low heat for 10–15 minutes; do not boil. Remove from the heat, and strain the lavender buds from the Half & Half. Discard the herbs. Return the Half & Half to the saucepan, and add the chocolate. Cook over low heat, stirring constantly, until the chocolate is completely melted. Add the vanilla extract, and stir well.

Serve in a mug, and top with a dollop of fresh whipped cream and shaved chocolate. For a more delicate fare, serve in teacups or cappuccino cups. Makes approximately 2 mug-size servings.

Chef's Comments

If you prefer a sweeter beverage, use milk chocolate chips instead.

Any "leftovers" can be refrigerated and reheated to enjoy the next day.

Variation

Be creative! Variations of this recipe can be made by simply substituting 1 1/2 tsp of your favorite extract for the vanilla.

For hot chocolate without comparison, try these extracts: mint, raspberry, almond, or coconut.

Photo Courtesy of Debbie Walter

Recipe Tested in the Kitchen of Debbie Walter

Chocolate Lavender Raspberry Jam

This jam is lovely on toast or biscuits and tastes absolutely amazing when spread over a fresh croissant. Although any variety of fruit can be used in this easy-to-make chocolate jam, my favorite is raspberry since it mingles so well with the lavender and chocolate.

8 1/2 cups fresh raspberries (about 2 pounds)

3 cups granulated sugar

2 Tbsp fresh-squeezed lemon juice

1 1/2 cups bittersweet chocolate chips

1 Tbsp Organic Culinary Lavender Buds

In a heavy-bottomed saucepan, mix together the raspberries, sugar, and lemon juice. Place the pan over medium heat, and simmer the mixture for about 5 minutes, stirring slowly—skim off any foam from the surface, if necessary. Remove from the heat, and set aside.

Add the chocolate chips and lavender buds to the raspberry mixture, and stir until the chocolate chips are completely melted. Spoon the mixture into a large bowl, and cover with parchment paper. Refrigerate overnight to allow the flavors to mature. Transfer the jam into airtight containers. The jam can be stored in the refrigerator for up to 1 month. For longer storage, place the airtight containers in the freezer for up to 3 months. The jam may also be kept in seal-tight jars—see the canning directions in the "Chef's" box to the right. Makes approximately 6 cups.

Chef's Comments

Directions for canning...

Heat 6 glass jam jars (8 oz. size) in boiling water for 5 minutes. Remove the jars from the water, and allow them to cool and dry. Return the raspberry mixture to a saucepan, and bring it to a simmer over medium heat for 10 minutes—skim off any foam from the surface, if necessary.

Remove the saucepan from the heat, and immediately fill the jars—use oven mitts to hold the jars because they will become very hot. Screw the covers onto the jars, turn them upside down, and allow them to cool overnight. Store the unopened jars, right side up, in a cool, dark place for up to 6 months. Once opened, store the jam in the refrigerator, and use within 1 month.

Photo Courtesy of Debbie Walter

Recipe Tested in the Kitchen of Debbie Walter

Lavender Chocolate-Covered Popcorn

Kids of all ages will enjoy this familiar yet enhanced confection. Lavender and two kinds of chocolate add both fun and flavor! It's bound to become an often-asked-for treat.

10 cups air-popped popcorn (without salt or butter)

1/4 cup honey

2 Tbsp butter

3/4 cup milk chocolate chips

1/4 cup semisweet chocolate chips

1 tsp kosher salt

1 tsp Organic Culinary Lavender Buds ·

1 cup chopped nuts (optional)

Place the popped corn on a large cookie sheet lined with parchment or waxed paper.

In a small saucepan, heat together the honey, butter, and milk chocolate chips over low heat, stirring until the chocolate is completely melted. Remove from the heat, and allow the honey and chocolate mixture to cool slightly. Pour the mixture over the popcorn, stirring to coat evenly. Cool to room temperature.

Once the chocolate has hardened on the popcorn, melt the semisweet chocolate chips in a small saucepan over low heat, stirring constantly. Drizzle the semisweet chocolate over the popcorn. Sprinkle with the kosher salt, lavender buds, and chopped nuts, if desired. Cool to room temperature once again, and then break into pieces. Enjoy!

Store in an airtight container for up to 1 week. Makes 10 cups.

Photo Courtesy of Laura Cesaro

Recipe Tested in the Kitchen of Laura Cesaro

Triple Chocolate Lavender Shortbread

What could possibly be better than chocolate shortbread? Why, chocolate shortbread with lavender, of course! These crisp and buttery shortbread cookies are made with a hint of lavender and then topped with layers of rich, luscious chocolate. Definitely not your average cookie, they taste as delectable as they look.

1 1/2 cups unsalted butter, softened

1 cup powdered (confectioners') sugar

2 Tbsp granulated sugar

1/4 cup unsweetened Dutch-process cocoa powder

1 1/2 tsp vanilla extract

1 Tbsp Organic Culinary Lavender Buds

1/4 tsp salt

3 cups all-purpose flour

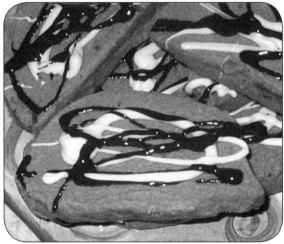

Photo Courtesy of Laura Cesaro

Topping

1 bar (3.5 oz. size) good-quality white chocolate, chopped (we prefer Lindt or Ghirardelli brands—use sweetened bars, not baking chocolate)

1 bar (3.5 oz. size) good-quality dark chocolate, chopped (we prefer Lindt or Ghirardelli brands—use sweetened bars, not baking chocolate)

In a medium-size mixing bowl, beat the butter with an electric mixer until light and fluffy. Add the powdered sugar, granulated sugar, cocoa powder, vanilla extract, lavender buds, and salt to the butter, and continue to beat for another 4–5 minutes. Continuing to use the electric mixer, slowly add the flour, one cup at a time, until well incorporated. If the dough is still sticky, add a touch more flour. Form the dough into 2 logs, each about 2 1/2–3 inches in diameter. Wrap the logs in plastic wrap, and refrigerate them until firm, about 1 hour.

Preheat the oven to 325°F. Slice the dough into 1/2-inch-thick slices. Lay the cookie slices on a parchment-lined baking sheet. Bake at 325° for 10–15 minutes or until the shortbread looks dry and feels firm to the touch. Allow the cookies to cool completely on wire racks.

In a microwave-safe bowl, melt the white chocolate in the microwave (at 50% power) in 30-second increments, stirring each time until smooth. In a different microwave-safe bowl, melt the dark chocolate in the microwave (at 50% power) in 30-second increments, stirring each time until smooth. Fit 2 pastry bags with 1/8-inch plain tips. Spoon the white chocolate into one of the pastry bags, and the dark chocolate into the other. —OR— Spoon the 2 chocolates into 2 different plastic freezer bags. When you are ready to use the chocolates, simply cut off a very small portion of a corner from each plastic bag.

Using either the pastry bags or the plastic bags, decoratively trim the cookies with the white and dark chocolates. Allow the chocolates to set for about 1 hour at room temperature. Store the shortbread in an airtight container in single layers between sheets of waxed paper. Makes approximately 3 dozen cookies.

Recipe Tested in the Kitchen of Laura Cesaro

Lavender Chocolate S'more "Stuffed" Cupcakes

Somehow, over the years, cupcakes have emerged as being one of the hottest bakery trends! From stuffed cupcakes to fanciful ones replacing the traditional wedding cake, the rage has spread like wildfire. Sure, cupcakes have always made everyone smile, but who knew that they would ever create such a terrific sensation? Cupcake mania has even captured my niece Kari, who dreams of one day owning her own little upscale cupcake café. Who knows, these Lavender Chocolate S'more "Stuffed" Cupcakes may end up being offered to Kari's customers someday! Until then, this decadent recipe should at least help curb your chocolate cravings.

1 stick butter, at room temperature
1 1/2 cups granulated sugar
2 large eggs, at room temperature
1 tsp vanilla extract
1 1/4 cups Half & Half
2 1/3 cups self-rising cake flour
1/3 cup unsweetened cocoa powder
(we prefer Hershey's special dark)
1 tsp Organic Culinary Lavender
Buds
Chocolate Ganache (see the recipe
on the next page)
1 1/2 cups marshmallow creme (for
stuffing)
1 1/2 cups teddy grahams (for
garnish)
1 1/2 cups mini-marshmallows (for
garnish)

Preheat the oven to 350°F. Line the insides of muffin tins with paper liners, and set aside.

Whip the butter with an electric mixer on medium speed until it is soft, and then add the sugar. Beat an additional 3 minutes until the butter and sugar are creamy. Gradually add the eggs, one at a time, and beat until smooth. Add the vanilla extract and Half & Half, a little at a time, and continue to beat until all of the ingredients are completely smooth and well blended.

In a separate bowl, sift together the flour and cocoa powder. Add 1/3 of the flour mixture to the moist ingredients, and mix on medium speed until smooth, scraping the sides of the bowl as needed. Repeat the addition of the flour twice more, scraping the sides of the bowl after each addition. Mix for 1 minute more after it is all incorporated. Then add the lavender buds, and beat on low speed until they are well mixed in.

Fill each of the cupcake liners 2/3 full, and bake at 350° for 15–20 minutes or until the cupcakes are golden brown on top and a toothpick inserted in the center comes out clean. Allow the cupcakes to cool completely on a wire rack before stuffing and frosting. Prepare the Chocolate Ganache.

With a small paring knife, cut a small cylinder out of the center of each cupcake, and set the cylinder aside. Spoon about 1 heaping tsp of marshmallow creme into the center of each cupcake, and place the cylinder cutout back into the cupcake. Once all of the cupcakes are stuffed with the marshmallow creme, top them with the prepared Chocolate Ganache, and garnish with 2 or 3 teddy grahams and a few mini-marshmallows. Makes approximately 18 cupcakes.

Chocolate Ganache

3/4 cup heavy whipping cream
2 Tbsp unsalted butter
2 cups bittersweet chocolate chips
1 tsp vanilla extract

In a small saucepan, bring the cream and butter to a boil over medium-high heat. Reduce the heat to low, and stir in the chocolate and vanilla extract. Continue to stir over low heat until the chocolate is melted and smooth. Remove from the heat. Allow the ganache to cool for at least 15 minutes. Stir well before frosting the cupcakes.

Recipe Tested in the Kitchen of Sharon & Kari Bacis

Rich Lavender Chocolate Lava Cakes

These luscious cakes are a medley of chocolate, caramel, and lavender, and whenever I make them, my friends and family always make sure they leave room for dessert.

2 1/2 sticks unsalted butter

3/4 cup bittersweet chocolate chips

2 Tbsp instant coffee OR instant espresso powder

2 tsp Organic Culinary Lavender Buds

1/2 tsp vanilla extract

4 eggs

1/2 cup granulated sugar

3/4 cup all-purpose flour

3 Tbsp evaporated milk, plus 1/4 cup, separated

16 caramel candies

Preheat the oven to 350°F. You will need enough muffin pans to give you 12 muffin cups. Spray the cups with nonstick cooking spray, or butter and flour the cups instead. In a microwave-safe bowl, melt together the butter and chocolate chips in the microwave (at 50% power) in 30-second increments, stirring each time until the chocolate is completely melted. Stir in the instant coffee (or espresso powder), lavender buds, and vanilla extract until the ingredients are well blended. Set aside.

In a separate bowl, mix together the eggs and sugar, and beat with an electric mixer for about 5 minutes on medium speed. Once the eggs and sugar are thickened, reduce the mixer's speed to low, and gradually add the flour. Beat on low until the ingredients are smooth. Add the chocolate mixture, and beat for about 3 minutes until the batter becomes thick and glossy. Fill the

Photo Courtesy of Jessica Criscenti

prepared muffin cups 2/3 full with the batter. Bake the cakes for 5 minutes at 350°.

While the cakes are baking, combine the 3 Tbsp of evaporated milk with the caramels in a microwave-safe bowl. Melt in the microwave in 20-second increments, stirring each time until the caramels are completely melted. (You can also melt the caramels using a double boiler.) After the cakes have baked for the 5 minutes, spoon 2 tsp of the caramel mixture into the center of each cake (you should have some caramel left over). Return the muffins to the oven, and bake for an additional 8 minutes.

Stir the 1/4 cup of evaporated milk into the remaining caramel mixture, and set aside. Remove the cakes from the oven, and allow them to cool for 3–5 minutes. Invert on a serving plate. Add your favorite ice cream, and then drizzle the remaining caramel topping over the top. Serve immediately. Makes approximately 12 lava cakes.

Recipe Tested in the Kitchen of Jessica Criscenti

Chocolate Lavender Bread Pudding

There are many opinions about bread pudding's origins, but a couple of things are pretty certain: it was known as "poor man's pudding" and it served a single purpose—to make use of stale bread. The addition of lavender and chocolate, though, transforms this humble dish into a scrumptious dessert, making it a truly delicious rags-to-riches story! Though it's unlikely that there will be any leftovers, it's also wonderful cold.

3 cups Half & Half

2 Tbsp Organic Culinary Lavender Buds

3 eggs

2 egg yolks

1 tsp vanilla extract

1/2 cup granulated sugar

1/2 tsp salt

1 cup semisweet chocolate chips

3 cups french bread, cut into cubes (bread should be day-old)

Butter an 8-inch x 8-inch baking pan. In a heavy saucepan, combine the Half & Half and lavender buds. Cook over medium-high heat until bubbles appear around the edge of the saucepan, but do not let it come to a boil. Remove from the heat, and allow the lavender buds to steep in the Half & Half for 30 minutes. Strain the lavender buds from the Half & Half, and discard the lavender buds. Return the Half & Half to the saucepan, and set aside.

In a medium-size mixing bowl, beat together the eggs, egg yolks, vanilla extract, sugar, and salt with an electric mixer until smooth. Reheat the Half & Half over medium heat just until it begins to bubble. Do not let it come to a boil. While constantly beating the egg and sugar combination with the mixer, slowly add the hot Half & Half.

Return the mixture to the saucepan, and cook over medium-low heat, stirring constantly, until the custard thickens slightly and coats the back of a spoon. Do not let the custard boil, or it will curdle. Add the chocolate, and using a wire whisk, stir until it melts. Remove from the heat, and set aside.

Place the bread cubes into the prepared baking pan. Pour the custard over the bread, evenly coating all of the cubes. Press the cubes down with a spatula. Cover with plastic wrap, and set aside. Allow the bread to absorb the custard for about 1 hour.

Preheat the oven to 350°F. Uncover the baking pan, and turn the bread cubes over, mixing again so that all of the bread is evenly coated with the custard. Bake, uncovered, at 350° for 35–45 minutes or until the edges are firm but the center still jiggles slightly. Cool for 10 minutes, and serve with fresh whipped cream. Refrigerate any leftovers. Makes approximately 6 servings.

Chef's Comments

It is best if the bread is day-old or left outside of its package overnight.

Recipe Tested in the Kitchen of Evelyn Bradley

Lavender Mint Brownies

I've always been a fan of brownies, but something magnificent happened when I added lavender and mint to my old-fashioned recipe. The rich Chocolate Mint Ganache, when poured over these brownies, gives them a whole new dimension. Mere words cannot describe their decadent texture. If you are a chocolate fanatic, these are definitely for you!

1 stick unsalted butter

1/3 cup bittersweet chocolate chips

3/4 cup granulated sugar

1 1/2 tsp Organic Culinary Lavender Buds, ground

1 tsp instant espresso powder OR instant coffee granules

2 large eggs, slightly beaten

1/2 tsp vanilla extract

1/4 tsp salt

1/3 cup all-purpose flour

Chocolate Mint Ganache (see the recipe to the right)

Preheat the oven to 325°F. Butter and flour an 8-inch square baking pan. In a large saucepan, heat the butter and chocolate chips over medium heat, stirring constantly, until the chocolate is completely

Chocolate Mint Ganache

1/4 cup heavy whipping cream

2 Tbsp unsalted butter

1/2 cup bittersweet chocolate chips

1 tsp granulated sugar

3/4 tsp natural mint extract

In a small saucepan, bring the cream and butter to a boil over medium-high heat. Add the chocolate, sugar, and mint extract. Remove from the heat, and stir until the sugar is completely dissolved and the chocolate is melted and smooth.

melted. Once it is melted, remove the pan from the heat, and add the sugar, ground lavender buds, espresso, eggs, vanilla extract, and salt. Beat the ingredients with an electric mixer on low speed until well blended.

Photo Courtesy of Jennifer Vasich

Fold in the flour, and stir just until blended. Spoon the batter into the prepared baking pan. Bake at 325° for 40 minutes or until a wooden toothpick inserted in the center comes out almost clean, with just a few crumbs clinging to it, but is not wet. Use caution not to over-bake. Remove the baking pan from the oven, and allow the brownies to cool. Meanwhile, prepare the Chocolate Mint Ganache. Allow the ganache to cool slightly, about 5 minutes, and then pour it over the brownies. Completely chill the brownies before cutting. Makes approximately 12 servings.

Chef's Comments

Ganache (gahn-AHSH) is a rich chocolate glaze made by melting together chocolate, whipping cream, and butter. It is one of the most simple yet versatile toppings you can make—try it on cakes, pies, and other desserts.

These brownies cut easier if you chill them slightly, but they taste better when served at room temperature. They are very rich, and we recommend cutting each 8-inch square baking pan into 12 brownies.

For a doubly chocolate delight, heat the brownies, and serve them with a scoop of Chocolate Lavender Custard, which can be found on page 292.

Recipe Tested in the Kitchen of Linda Mascagni

Dark Chocolate Lavender Raspberry Truffles

It is said that these irresistible sweets are called truffles because they resemble the truffle fungus—a gourmet delicacy similar to a mushroom—which can be found growing around the roots of trees in France and Italy. Chocolate truffles are usually formed into misshapen balls and rolled in cocoa powder—perhaps to echo the wild truffle's shape and "woodsy" appearance. These rich truffles are great to give as gifts—but even better to keep for yourself.

1/2 cup heavy whipping cream, plus 1 Tbsp

2 Tbsp Organic Culinary Lavender Buds

2 cups bittersweet chocolate chips (we find that Ghirardelli's 60% cacao
   bittersweet chocolate chips work best)

1 1/2 sticks unsalted butter, cut into small pieces

3/4 tsp raspberry extract

2/3 cup unsweetened cocoa

In a stainless steel saucepan, heat the cream over medium-high heat just until the cream begins to bubble. Remove the cream from the heat, and stir in the lavender buds. Allow to steep for 15 minutes. Strain the lavender buds from the cream. Set the cream aside, and discard the lavender buds.

In a microwave-safe bowl, melt together the chocolate, butter, and lavender-infused cream in the microwave (at 50% power) in 30-second increments, stirring each time until smooth. After the chocolate is completely melted, add the raspberry extract, and blend until smooth. Pour the chocolate mixture into a shallow dish. Cool, cover, and refrigerate until firm, at least 2 hours or overnight.

On parchment paper or a pie plate, spread the cocoa powder evenly. Line an airtight container with parchment or waxed paper. Dip a melon baller or small spoon into a glass of warm water, wipe dry with a clean kitchen towel, and scrape across the surface of the chilled truffle mixture to form a rough 1-inch ball. Drop the ball into the cocoa. Repeat with the remaining truffle mixture. Gently roll the truffles to evenly coat them with the cocoa powder.

Transfer the truffles to the airtight container, separating the layers with additional parchment or waxed paper. Truffles can be refrigerated in an airtight container for up to 2 weeks or kept in the freezer for up to 3 months.

Makes approximately 3 1/2 dozen truffles.

Photo Courtesy of Jessica Criscenti

Photo Courtesy of Jennifer Vasich

Recipe Tested in the Kitchen of Jessica Criscenti

Lavender & Walnut "Mackinac Island" Fudge

Located in northern Michigan, beautiful Mackinac Island is well known for its tempting fudge. Residents and merchants on the island lovingly refer to the tourists who indulge in their famous confection as "fudgies." To give us a taste of the North without the four-hour drive, I created my own "Mackinac Island" fudge. This recipe is reminiscent of the island's delectable confections, but the added lavender makes it even more enjoyable.

1/4 cup heavy whipping cream

1/4 cup milk

1/2 cup unsalted butter

1/2 cup packed light brown sugar

1/2 cup granulated sugar

1/8 tsp sea salt

1 tsp vanilla extract

1 1/3 cups powdered (confectioners') sugar

2/3 cup Dutch-process cocoa powder

1/2 cup milk chocolate chips

1/2 cup walnuts, chopped

1 Tbsp Organic Culinary Lavender Buds

Prepare a baking pan to hold the fudge by buttering the bottom and sides of the pan or lining it with parchment paper.

In a heavy saucepan, mix together the cream, milk, butter, brown sugar, granulated sugar, and salt. Cook over medium heat, and bring to a boil, stirring constantly. Reduce the heat to low, and simmer for about 6 minutes. Stirring constantly again, add the vanilla extract, powdered sugar, and cocoa powder.

Remove the saucepan from the heat. With an electric mixer on low speed, beat the mixture until thick. Pour the fudge into the prepared baking pan, and spread it out evenly.

In a microwave-safe bowl, melt the chocolate chips in the microwave (at 50% power) in 30-second increments, stirring each time until smooth. Fold in the nuts and lavender buds.

Pour the melted chocolate over the fudge already in the baking pan, and swirl together. Place the fudge in the freezer for 20 minutes. Once the fudge is set, cut into pieces.

The fudge may be stored in an airtight container and refrigerated for up to 2 weeks. Makes approximately 1 pound.

Recipe Tested in the Kitchen of Leah Dzierzawski

Aztec Spiced Lavender Chocolates

Spicy yet sweet, these artisan chocolates are flavored with cinnamon and cayenne pepper! Those ingredients may seem like strange additions to chocolate, but in fact, the ancient Maya and Aztecs of Mesoamerica used to add chili peppers, among other things, to their chocolate. A hint of orange offers a nice complement to the dark chocolate, and the sunflower seeds and lavender add a little crunch. A truly exotic and surprisingly tasteful confection, these chocolates taste best when made with the finest gourmet chocolate you can find. We prefer Belgian chocolate; however, Swiss chocolate works wonderfully too.

16 oz. Belgian dark chocolate (at least 60% cacao), finely chopped or grated

1/2 tsp cinnamon

1/4 tsp cayenne pepper

1 tsp orange extract

1 tsp Organic Culinary Lavender Buds

1/4 cup sunflower seeds

chocolate candy molds (we prefer 1 oz. petit four molds since these
    chocolates are so rich, but any candy mold will do)

In a microwave-safe bowl, melt the chocolate in the microwave (at 50% power) in 30-second increments, stirring each time until the chocolate is completely melted. Add the cinnamon, cayenne pepper, and orange extract. Stir until all of the spices are well distributed. Fold in the lavender buds and sunflower seeds, and stir well.

Using a spoon, slowly fill each mold, or pour the chocolate into each mold from a measuring cup. With a table knife or spatula, scrape off any excess chocolate into a clean bowl; it can be gently warmed and reused. When the back of the mold is smooth and even, gently tap the tray of chocolates on the countertop to pop any air bubbles.

Place the chocolate mold in the freezer, and allow it to harden. Once the chocolate is firm enough to come out of the mold, invert the entire mold onto a cookie sheet lined with parchment paper, and twist gently to release the chocolates. Makes approximately 2 dozen 1-inch square pieces.

Chef's Comments

If you don't have a chocolate mold, you may make this chocolate into a "bark." Simply pour the melted chocolate on a cookie sheet lined with parchment paper, place it in the freezer to harden, and score the chocolate with a knife. Then break it into bite-size pieces.

We usually purchase our Belgian chocolate from www.chocolatesource.com.

Photo Courtesy of Nancy Feldbush

Recipe Tested in the Kitchen of Maryanne MacLeod

Lavender Chocolate Fondue with Fresh Fruit Kebobs

Some friends gave us a fondue pot for our wedding. After hosting our first fondue party, we were instant fans. This Lavender Chocolate Fondue is quick and easy to make—and always a popular choice. Our favorite chocolate for this recipe is a dark Belgian chocolate; however, any chocolate may be used. We prefer using fruit with our fondue, but yummy dipping alternatives include pound cake, marshmallows, and pretzels.

16 oz. dark or bittersweet Belgian chocolate (we prefer Callebaut brand)

1 cup heavy whipping cream

2 Tbsp Organic Culinary Lavender Buds

1/2 cup (4 oz.) cream cheese, cut into chunks

1 Tbsp amaretto extract

Fresh Fruit Kebobs (see the recipe on the
    next page)

Chef's Comments

We usually purchase our Belgian chocolate from www.chocolatesource.com.

Break the chocolate into small pieces, and set aside. In a medium-size saucepan, combine the cream and lavender buds. Bring the mixture to a boil over medium-high heat. Once the cream begins to boil, immediately reduce the heat to low. Simmer for 5 minutes, stirring occasionally and using caution not to scald the cream. Remove from the heat, and strain the lavender buds from the cream. Discard the lavender buds, and return the cream to the saucepan. Add the chocolate, cream cheese, and amaretto extract to the cream, and stir over low heat until completely smooth. Pour the chocolate mixture into a heated fondue pot, and serve with Fresh Fruit Kebobs or other dipping items. Makes approximately 6–8 servings.

Fresh Fruit Kebobs

1 pint fresh strawberries, stemmed and washed (cut large strawberries
    in half)

2 Granny Smith apples, peeled, cored, and cubed

4 cups fresh pineapple, peeled, cored, and cubed

2 cups honeydew melon, scooped into melon balls

2 kiwifruits, peeled and sliced

1 lemon

6-inch bamboo skewers

Place the fruit chunks on a large tray. Cut and squeeze the lemon over
the apple pieces to prevent them from browning. Alternating the fruits,
thread them onto the 6-inch bamboo skewers. Serve the fruit kabobs
with the Lavender Chocolate Fondue. Makes approximately 24 kabobs.

Photo Courtesy of Maryanne MacLeod

Recipe Tested in the Kitchen of Maryanne MacLeod

Recipe Index

Moose Run™
Productions

A publisher of books that offer readers a wholesome and enjoyable respite.

Moose Run Productions publishes books of various genres that are wholesome, decent, and uplifting.

If you would like a **free** copy of our catalog, please visit our Web site at moose-run.com or complete and send this form to:

Moose Run Productions • P.O. Box 46281 • Mount Clemens, Michigan 48046-6281

Name _____

Address _____

City, State, Zip _____

E-Mail (optional) _____